Forewor

BY ALISON MEC.
CEO, ENDSLEI<

MOST of us have heard the phrase '   _ .. *inevitable; change is constant*' (Benjamin Disraeli) but not many of us have considered the fact that successful change is not an inevitability, proven by a study showing that 88% of change initiatives fail!

Why? Because change is personal, not a process.

It is about people, like you and me, and how each of us views the world from our own perspective. The good news is that because change is personal, each of us has the personal power to change.

Endsleigh has worked closely with Campbell Macpherson over the past year to define a new strategic direction that will help us all to change in order to recapture Endsleigh's winning position. This book, *The Power to Change*, will give you the tools and approaches to embrace and celebrate change at both a personal and professional level. By using a unique approach that allows its readers to understand and engage with change on an emotional level, the book empowers us to identify our fears and doubts and to put change into perspective; enabling us to embrace the opportunities that change presents.

I was nine years of age when I first discovered what change meant for me. My parents moved abroad (to Cyprus, it wasn't all that bad…). It was a 'burning platform' kind of change that was done to me leaving behind familiarity, friends and a known future. This kind of change forced me to learn things about myself: that I am curious about the unfamiliar, that I love new challenges, that I am resilient, that I can change. Not that I knew any of that at nine years old, but they are traits that I now understand and that understanding has helped me to not just survive what life throws at me, but to find opportunities from the inevitable changes – and thrive. That's my story. We all have one, and I would encourage you to use the tips and techniques in this book to discover your change story.

2020 can only be described as the Year of Change. Covid-19 has been like a tsunami creating an adrenalin-fuelled surge and when we reflect on it, we realise that we have embraced and demonstrated amazing resilience to cope with change. As a business we've learnt a lot: the importance of our customers, our people, our partners and of digital connectivity. That sustainability isn't just about the environment, it's about human relationships, customer relationships, a solid strategic direction and financial security.

And so it feels appropriate that Endsleigh's new strategy is about all those things. Our growth strategy is about recapturing Endsleigh's position as *the* student insurer brand. It is about becoming the number one insurer for the education community. Persistency and customer loyalty lie at the core of the new strategy. It is about creating an A-Grade customer experience and delivering innovative propositions. It is about commercialising our strategic access partners. It is about re-creating a culture of enjoyment, accountability and innovation. It is about delivery.

We will achieve this by refocusing our business on our customers, our people and our partners to acquire new business from core markets and retain more customers. Endsleigh was founded by the ambition to create its own category when, in 1965, the NUS created insurance solutions for 'uninsurable' students, so it is our ambition to recapture that *Category of One* position by knowing and servicing our student and educational establishments better than anyone else.

The ambition we have will change our business and it will change us. It will take hard work, bravery, and a quantum leap of faith. But it will be worth it to recapture Endsleigh's greatness – not just surviving but thriving in a Category of One with a mission to protect students.

I am personally committed to set the business, and all of us, up to succeed by enabling us all to be a bit bolder and a bit braver in finding a 'Path to Yes'. To peel back some of what does not add value and get organised around a new Endsleigh. An Endsleigh that has clear accountability and goals, more collaborative successes and more effective processes and prioritisation to set us all up for success as we enter into this exciting new phase of growth for *Our Endsleigh*.

As with all change – personal or professional – embracing this new direction and being part of the growth of Our Endsleigh will require a leap of faith. While our strategy is designed for success, it is not designed for perfection, so we need every person to be on board and pulling in the same direction. I hope that you find the words, tools and insights from this book inspirational to identify your change story, to help you embrace change at work and in life, and to become the very best version of you.

Alison

PS

A final consideration from a couple of thought-provoking phrases I found in this book:

Every upside has a downside. Every silver lining has a cloud. Every decision comes with its own set of consequences. Those of us who can cope with change will survive. Those of us who are able to embrace change and look for the opportunities will thrive. And the power to change lies within every single one of us.

Praise for *The Power to Change*

Embracing change has never been so important. This book shows you how! SOPHIE DEVONSHIRE, CEO, THE MARKETING SOCIETY, AND AUTHOR OF *SUPERFAST: LEAD AT SPEED*

Invaluable advice on building the resilience we all need to embrace and deliver real change. DR BRONWYN KING AO, FOUNDER, TOBACCO FREE PORTFOLIOS

People like the idea of change but don't want to be changed. This book has the power to transform victims of change into change champions. JEREMY SNAPE, CEO, SPORTING EDGE, AND FORMER ENGLAND CRICKETER

This book will give you and your people the power to welcome change and look for the opportunities. PHIL VERITY, SENIOR PARTNER, MAZARS UK

The Power to Change

How to harness change to make it work for you

Campbell Macpherson

KoganPage

Publisher's note

Every possible effort has been made to ensure that the information contained in this book is accurate at the time of going to press, and the publisher and author cannot accept responsibility for any errors or omissions, however caused. No responsibility for loss or damage occasioned to any person acting, or refraining from action, as a result of the material in this publication can be accepted by the editor, the publisher or the author.

First published in Great Britain and the United States in 2021 by Kogan Page Limited

2nd Floor, 45 Gee Street	122 W 27th St, 10th Floor	4737/23 Ansari Road
London	New York, NY 10001	Daryaganj
EC1V 3RS	USA	New Delhi 110002
United Kingdom		India

www.koganpage.com

Kogan Page books are printed on paper from sustainable forests.

© Change & Strategy International Ltd, 2021

The right of Change & Strategy International Ltd to be identified as the author of this work has been asserted by them in accordance with the Copyright, Designs and Patents Act 1988.

ISBNs

Hardback	978 1 78966 496 6
Paperback	978 1 78966 495 9
eBook	978 1 78966 498 0

British Library Cataloguing-in-Publication Data

A CIP record for this book is available from the British Library.

Library of Congress Cataloging-in-Publication Data

Names: Macpherson, Campbell, 1963- author.
Title: The power to change : how to harness change to make it work for you / Campbell Macpherson.
Description: London, United Kingdom ; New York, NY : Kogan Page, [2021] | Includes bibliographical references and index. |
Identifiers: LCCN 2020033363 (print) | LCCN 2020033364 (ebook) | ISBN 9781789664959 (paperback) | ISBN 9781789664966 (hardback) | ISBN 9781789664980 (ebook)
Subjects: LCSH: Organizational change. | Change (Psychology)
Classification: LCC HD58.8 .M2226 2020 (print) | LCC HD58.8 (ebook) | DDC 650.1–dc23

Typeset by Integra Software Services, Pondicherry
Print production managed by Jellyfish
Printed and bound by CPI Group (UK) Ltd, Croydon CR0 4YY

'Change happens' as Forrest Gump should have said.

Those of us who can cope with change will survive.

Those of us who are able to embrace change
and look for the opportunities
will thrive.

And the power to change
lies within every single one of us.

Contents

About the author

Campbell Macpherson is an author, motivational keynote speaker, international business adviser, executive coach, workshop facilitator, Non-Executive Director and self-titled Change Catalyst. He is also an executive fellow of the world-renowned Henley Business School.

He runs highly acclaimed 'Leading Change' and 'Embracing Change' workshops for organizations worldwide, using key insights from his first book, *The Change Catalyst*, 2018 Business Book of the Year, and this book, *The Power to Change*.

Campbell has been enabling leaders to clarify their strategy, build cultures that embrace change and lead the successful instigation of sustainable change for more than 25 years as an internal change leader or external adviser for organizations large and small across the UK, Europe, Australia, United States, Asia and the Middle East.

His CV is nothing but change, with a myriad of jobs and a multitude of careers across a vast array of disciplines. He sold computers for NCR in the 1980s and ran his own multimedia company in the 1990s. He was a Senior Change Manager for Andersen Consulting, Head of eBusiness for the AMP Group, the inaugural Marketing Director of Virgin Wines, HR and Board Director of a 1,000-employee financial services advisory firm, Strategy Director of Zurich Global Life Emerging Markets and a senior adviser to the Abu Dhabi Investment Authority, one of the world's largest sovereign wealth funds.

He also flew jets (really badly) in the Royal Australian Air Force. He has a Physics degree from Melbourne University and was educated at a state school in Queensland, Australia; a school that majored in two main things – teenage pregnancies and surfing, neither of which he was particularly skilled at.

What drives him is a burning desire to help organizations and people to change.

He is a firm believer in 'Responsible Capitalism': that companies that exist solely for the financial gain of their executives and the creation of value for their shareholders will ultimately fail. To thrive in the long term, businesses must address the needs of all of their stakeholders (customers, employees, suppliers, partners and the communities in which they operate as well as shareholders and executives).

And the most important component of any organization is its people. People are the source of a company's competitive advantage and the drivers of change in any organization. Because all change is personal. Even the largest organizational change programme is actually the culmination of a plethora of individual, personal changes.

Campbell also strongly believes that none of us is powerless in the face of change. Even when change is done *to* us, we always have a choice. At the very least, we can choose how we react to the change – and this can make all the difference.

Campbell has had 20 different employers and has been made redundant three times. He spent his first 35 years in Australia before moving to the UK in 1999. He has lived as an expat in Abu Dhabi. He has moved house 18 times.

He is a sought-after speaker worldwide and travels the globe helping leaders to lead change and individuals to embrace change via his consultancy, Change & Strategy International (www.changeandstrategy.com).

Strangely, with all this change, Campbell has been married to the same wonderful woman since 1992 and has two truly remarkable adult children. He lives in Oxfordshire and divides his time between the UK, Australia and wherever his clients need him to be.

www.campbellmacphersonauthor.com

Preface
The pandemic that changed our world

On an unknown day in 2019, in a bustling 'wet market' in Wuhan, China, where caged wildlife co-existed with a slew of slaughtered and soon-to-be-slaughtered animals of all varieties, a flu-like virus seems to have leapt from a pangolin to a human. Most likely, the pangolin was infected by a bat – a species that previously gave us SARS, MERS and Ebola.

We humans have zero natural immunity to this new coronavirus – COVID-19 as it has been named – and as we now know, it is highly contagious and potentially fatal for our elderly and those of us with underlying health conditions.

The economic, social and personal impact of COVID-19 has been profound and, given the extent of the global reaction, its effects are likely to be felt for some time to come. It has changed our world in ways that we are yet to grasp fully.

It wreaked havoc with our economies, pushing countless businesses to the brink and beyond. Many of us lost our jobs or our incomes dried up. Governments around the world implemented desperate support measures, unheard of in peacetime. Government and corporate debt skyrocketed. Health systems were overwhelmed. Police and emergency services were overstretched. Airports were transformed into desolate wastelands. Train carriages, offices, restaurants and bars emptied.

We quickly learnt how to work from home and, through trial and error, discovered the tips and tricks on how to use video conferencing effectively. Necessity being the mother of invention and all that.

We fought one another over toilet rolls and rallied to help elderly neighbours.

We were encouraged and even forced to self-isolate – with the very alien absence of the face-to-face social interaction that we humans crave. We self-isolated with our partners and families, enduring a prolonged form of close contact that was previously only reserved for Christmas.

COVID-19 pushed our national and personal anxiety levels through the roof, inflamed by a 24/7 news industry that lurches from providing a much-needed social service to displaying an almost palpable delight in catastrophizing every new and uncertain development.

We are still uncertain about who to trust, who to believe or what to believe. We loathe uncertainty; it makes us fear the worst. The added problem with this pandemic is that we don't know how long it will last. Uncertainty topped with even more uncertainty.

It is the most perfect example of 'Burning Platform' change that we may ever witness; a common phenomenon that we discuss in detail in Chapters 10 and 11 – big change that has been done to us. And through this crisis we have all ridden the emotional roller-coaster that is the 'Burning Platform Change Curve'. We have experienced shock, denial, anger, fear and even depression. Several times.

The good news is, these emotions are normal. It is how we react to change. The trick is to acknowledge them, understand them and start to use them to our own advantage; to assess our situation, embrace the new reality and look for the opportunities. Because opportunities exist even in times of boundless uncertainty and massive disruption.

This virus has also given us a gift if we wish to receive it; a gift that is relevant for nations, corporations and individuals alike. It has given us a once-in-a-lifetime opportunity to reflect on what is important; to reflect on what it is we need to change.

It has forced us to question some of the key premises that, as a society, we seem to have taken for granted. The most important duty of any government is to keep its people safe. But safe from what? For millennia, governments have assumed that the greatest threat to their citizens was a physical attack from another nation, and globally they have ploughed trillions into weapons and military might, arguably at the expense of far more important aspects of our national and personal security.

While no health system could have been completely prepared for the speed and extent of this pandemic, some public health systems entered this crisis with a massive shortage of equipment, nurses, doctors and hospital beds. Privatized health systems have also been found wanting – and morally questionable. Aged care services, too, have been neglected. Too many people have died untested and untreated at home.

It has forced us to rethink how businesses work. Too many business models operate on the thinnest of margins and were therefore thrown into this crisis without a financial buffer. They had no choice but to cut staff to stay afloat. Not all will survive.

Have our governments and our systems of commerce been prioritizing the wrong things? This time it isn't just the banks that are asking for bail-outs. Airlines (public and private), railways, retailers, coffee shops, restaurants, pubs, manufacturers, big businesses, small businesses, sole traders and service providers of all persuasions have been in dire need of government cash.

And yet amid all this gloom, the air quality in the world's cities has improved dramatically. Globally, 4 million people have been dying from the effects of air pollution every year, according to the World Health Organization. The US National Academy of Sciences thinks the number could be twice that figure. The pause in manufacturing and the reduction in the number of cars on the roads due to COVID-19 may have saved tens of thousands of lives. How ironic.

Instinctively, we hope that change has an end date; that we can soon get back to the way things were. But what if we can't? What if we shouldn't?

This virus has forced massive change upon us all. We are all its victims. None of us has asked for it. None of us has asked for its consequences either. Like any big change that is forced upon us, we feel powerless in the face of such dramatic disruption. But we aren't powerless. We have the power to pause, reflect, reassess our priorities and identify what is truly important in our lives.

And then we can change.

This book is designed to help us do precisely that.

Acknowledgements

I loved writing this book. I loved researching it, discovering innumerable new insights along the way. I loved drafting it and redrafting it countless times. I loved interviewing fascinating people on the subject of change. I loved using my 'Leading Change' and 'Embracing Change' workshop delegates as guinea pigs as I was refining the content.

This book is the ying to *The Change Catalyst*'s yang. My first book was about leading change. This is about embracing it. It is for everyone.

The first thank you must go to Lucy Carragher, organizer of the Business Book of the Year Awards in London, who kindly asked me to be the keynote speaker at the 2019 awards gala dinner. I had a wonderful evening – as the videos of the night amply demonstrate! That was the night I met Helen Kogan, MD of Kogan Page, whom I am very proud to say is the publisher of *The Power to Change*. Thank you to Helen and Chris Cudmore for believing in the book and for believing in me. I look forward to a lengthy and fruitful relationship with their fabulous publishing house.

Thanks also to my agent, Jonathan Hayden. *The Power to Change* is the first collaboration between us and we are already working on the next two. I envisage we will be working together for a very long time to come.

Thank you to Dr Bronwyn King AO, founder of Tobacco Free Portfolios, for being so generous with her time. Her story of how she and her team encourages and enables investment companies to stop investing in or financing tobacco is genuinely inspirational, as is Bronwyn, and I am sure that Chapter 13 will leave you both inspired and stunned. Thank you also to Hannah Hickman of HENRY, another deeply inspiring organization that tackles childhood obesity by helping parents to change. There is also much to learn from HENRY's story in Chapter 24.

Thanks also to the always-smiling Douglas Fraser who did me the favour of proofreading, editing and providing new insights for Chapter 3: 'Climate Change: the dangerous power of denial'. Who better to whip that into shape than a clever young recent master's graduate in Environmental Policy and Management?!

Lastly, a gigantic thank you to my incredible wife and life-long partner, Jane, who would often enquire as to how my 'wisdom dispensing' was going and proofread the final draft, proclaiming, 'I love it. It's better than the first book'.

I'll take that.

Introduction

Coping with change is one of the most important skills that any of us can hone. This book will help you to go even further. It will help you to embrace change. It will give you the power to change.

Change is tough. Most of us feel utterly powerless when confronted by it – especially big change that happens *to* us such as losing a job, becoming divorced or the death of a loved one. But we are not powerless. We can learn to turn situations to our own advantage. We all have the power to embrace the change and look for opportunities – we just need to be able to harness it.

Every one of us copes with small changes on a daily basis. We accept them, adapt and get on with our day. We have all dealt with innumerable changes throughout our lives – some that have been thrust upon us and some we have chosen to instigate ourselves. When change is forced upon us, we can feel helpless, that we are not in control. But we are completely in control of one vital thing – how we choose to react to the change – and this choice can put us in the driver's seat. It can make all the difference.

Even change we bring about ourselves can be tough, as all change requires giving up something – even 'good' change. And there is always a little part of us that wants to cling on to those things we are letting go – to stick with the old mobile rather than jump into the world of the smartphone; to remain in the same team at work; to stay in the same neighbourhood; to stay in a boring job or a loveless relationship because it's 'better the devil you know'.

This book is the result of almost 30 years of helping organizations and individuals lead change, cope with change and embrace change. It is the result of helping leaders question their strategy, clarify their strategy and align their organizations to deliver. It is the result of helping leadership teams to buy companies, merge companies and dispose of companies while looking after their people along the way. It is the result of reorganizing and restructuring organizations. It is the result of helping small- and medium-sized companies to grow. It is the result of transforming departments and helping leaders to transform their leadership teams.

It is the result of helping people to pause, reflect, embrace the new, seek out the opportunities – and thrive. It is the result of having experienced countless personal changes in my own life. Because change is inevitable.

Three of the key lessons I have learnt from all of this are:

1 All change is personal. Even the most significant corporate transformation is actually the sum of countless personal changes across the organization.
2 All change is emotional. We humans are emotional beings. When it comes to change, emotion trumps logic every single time.
3 No-one embraces change simply because they are told to do so. We only change if and when we want to. (How many social workers does it take to change a light bulb? Only one, but the light bulb has to want to change.)

When it comes to change, emotion trumps logic every single time.

My previous book on this fascinating topic, *The Change Catalyst: Secrets to successful and sustainable business change*, was awarded the title of 2018 Business Book of the Year. It is about leading change: a how-to manual for leaders to lead successful change. It explains in detail how successful organizational change is all about people:

> Only your people can deliver your strategy. Only your people can deliver the change your business requires.

This book, *The Power to Change*, is for everyone. It is a guide to help you cope with personal change of all shapes and sizes – and ultimately to embrace change, harnessing it for your own benefit.

Part One explores our rapidly changing world. It discusses some of the key technological changes that are transforming the way we live and the way we work. Neither will ever be the same again. We explore artificial intelligence (Terminator or Liberator?), the Internet of Things (IOT), 3-D printing, political change, social change, how human lifespans are increasing, climate change, Boyan Slat and the Millennials… the amount of change coming our way could either be seen as frightening or full of opportunity. It is entirely up to us.

Part Two explores the psychology of change, particularly the power of emotion and the pivotal role it plays in our decision-making and our ability to embrace change. I use the challenge of losing weight as an example of the battle between logic and emotion that rages within all of us – and something that two-thirds of us in the West battle with to varying degrees.

Part Three is about the different types of change and our natural, instinctive reactions to them. You will be introduced to the Change Matrix and the Change Curves. I have included some rather frank and personal reflections of my journey through the 'Burning Platform Change Curve' (how we react to big change that is done to us) and detailed the fascinating and inspirational story of Dr Bronwyn King's journey through the 'Quantum Leap Change Curve' (big change that we instigate ourselves) in her quest to convince the world's largest pension funds and asset managers to stop investing in tobacco – a product that kills more people in a month than war, drugs, crime and guns combined kill in a year.

Part Four details the personal, and emotional obstacles to change that we place in our own path and, more importantly, discusses ways we can overcome them. I also explore the power of yoga to help with personal change – with assistance from my wife, Jane, who happens to be one of the most intuitive and empathetic yoga teachers you could ever have the fortune to meet.

Part Five expands upon this critical theme and explores additional strategies and tools you can put into practice to 'Be your own Change Catalyst'. We explore the concept of resilience and ways to develop it, the importance of creating favourable conditions for change (featuring the childhood obesity charity HENRY), finding the help you need, helping others, developing your own personal SWOT and strategic plan, and treating yourself like a change project.

Then it is all summed up and tied into a neat bow in Part Six, 'The secrets to embracing change'.

The book is designed to give us the power to change – to make the most of changes that are thrust upon us; and to seek out and embrace change that will help us grow and improve our lives for the better.

I hope it does precisely this for you and that you enjoy your immersion in *The Power to Change*.

Campbell
www.campbellmacphersonauthor.com

PART ONE

Our rapidly changing world

*Change is inevitable; change
is constant.* BENJAMIN DISRAELI[1]

Disraeli obviously wasn't the first public figure to speak of change. Far
from it. Aristotle wrote about it constantly more than 2,000 years
before him. 'Change in all things is sweet' was among the many comments
he penned on the subject. Change was also central to many of Buddha's
thoughts and teachings: 'Everything changes, nothing remains without
change.'

But you don't have to be a two-time British Prime Minister, the father of
Ancient Greek philosophy or the very first Buddhist monk to know that
change is inevitable. We all know this. We live it every day. Change is a fact
of life that we all have no choice but to deal with. Those of us who are able
to acknowledge this fact and cope with change will survive. Those who are
able to seek out change – and actively embrace it – will thrive.

Disraeli, Aristotle and Buddha would have been blown away by the change we now witness today on a daily basis. What they couldn't possibly have foreseen is the incredible rate at which the pace of change would accelerate in the 21st century.

The breadth of changes the world witnessed in the last half of the 20th century was breathtaking – from antibiotics to television, computers, putting a man on the moon and the internet. However, last century's changes almost pale in comparison to the amount of change we have all adapted to during the first 20 years of this millennium.

But to quote the rock group, Bachman Turner Overdrive, 'We ain't seen nothin' yet'.[2]

Bill Gates, founder of Microsoft, once said that we tend to over-estimate the impact of change that will occur over the next two to three years and under-estimate the change that we will experience over the next 10 years. This has never been truer: the most dramatic changes are yet to come. The way we work, the way we live, how long we live, the kind of societies we live in... will simply never be the same again. There is a tsunami of unprecedented change heading our way.

We simply have no choice but to get ready for it...

CHAPTER ONE

The technology revolution

I think there is a world market for maybe five computers. THOMAS WATSON, FOUNDER OF IBM IN 1943

Technology is disrupting entire industries, decimating swathes of traditional jobs and creating brand new occupations at a speed that we have never seen before. Every industry, every business, every job and every one of us is being affected.

Technology is also enabling us to live longer – much longer. It may even help us to save the planet from the environmental destruction we have wreaked upon it. These changes are already starting to precipitate a crisis in both capitalism and government as the world's leaders struggle with the challenges of how to fund a population that is living longer yet working less within societies that are becoming increasingly polarized. Each one of these momentous changes has already begun, and while some of them are more than a little worrying, they will also create new and exciting opportunities for those of us able to seek out and embrace the change.

To prepare for change, we first need to understand what is heading our way. Then we can start to analyse how we are likely to be affected – and what we can do to take full advantage of the opportunities.

Being forewarned is forearmed. So, let's take a little peek at just some of the tech-induced developments that are changing our world forever.

The web we weave

Little more than a quarter of a century ago, in the 1990s, the internet escaped from the US military and was introduced to the world. People started to build web pages. The rest of us couldn't understand why. Today, the internet is ubiquitous and it has been responsible for the birth and rebirth of some of the world's largest corporations.

Eight of the world's largest 10 companies are tech firms, the top four worth $5.5 trillion+, including Apple and Microsoft, who reinvented themselves upon the arrival of the world wide web and Alphabet/Google, Amazon, Facebook, Alibaba and Tencent, who owe their very existence to the commercialization of the internet. Together, these corporations have not only transformed the stock markets, they have transformed our lives.

Netflix, Amazon and Apple have destroyed the video industry and transformed film and television production worldwide. They have changed the way we consume films, documentaries and television forever.

Amazon has transformed retail throughout the West. Our shopping malls and Main Streets are struggling to adapt. Many never will.

Apple and Google have transformed the phone into the most powerful hand-held (and wearable) device we could have possibly imagined.

From its humble beginnings as a search engine, Google is changing the world.

Microsoft has miraculously reinvented itself twice in its 40-year history. It is now a cloud company competing with the likes of Amazon and Alibaba to provide the world's largest companies with cloud-based storage and services.

Tencent and Alibaba are the Google and Amazon of China.

LinkedIn, purchased by Microsoft for a mere US $26 billion, has upended the recruitment industry. The comparative advantage of the head-hunting industry used to be their databases and network – recruiters knew the names and numbers of all the key people in a certain company. Today, anyone with a LinkedIn account can find this out in minutes via their phones.

The end of truth?

The truth has become subjective and elusive. We used to reach for the august tomes of the *Encyclopaedia Britannica* if we needed to discover the truth about a particular topic. Now we reach for our phones only to be bombarded by untold versions of the 'truth' from every possible angle and perspective. By making information available to everyone, the internet was supposed to have unleashed truth to the world. Unfortunately the truth has been lost among an avalanche of opinions. Elections are influenced by stealthy data manipulators such as Cambridge Analytica and AggregateIQ serving up blatant misinformation directly to our Facebook and Twitter feeds. The latest US President uses Twitter as his broadcast medium of choice, making an average of 22 untrue statements every single day.[1] On 26 April 2019, President Donald Trump's tally of lies, untruths and distortion of facts since assuming office raced past the 10,000 mark. By mid 2020, that number had raced past 20,000. News agencies report his tweets, often without checking the facts, and the untruth takes on a life of its own. 'If you repeat a lie often enough, people will believe it, and you will even come to believe it yourself.'[2] To be fair to the news agencies, the untruths come so thick and fast, there is almost no time to disprove the first one before the next dozen have landed!

The Internet of Things

The award for the coolest title in the tech world today goes to the Internet of Things, or IOT. From lights and home heating you can switch on and off remotely from your iPhone, fridges that tell you when you are running out of milk, to machine parts that tell you when they need replacing – IOT is infiltrating every aspect of our lives. IOT is changing every industry. It is baked into buildings, roads, bridges, power stations, water treatment plants, council playgrounds, everything.

The ubiquity of IOT hit me when I was designing a 'Leading Change' programme for a 'water supply and disposal' company. Basically, they make pipes. In the planning call with the client, I asked what they thought were the biggest challenges in their industry and their instant reply was 'digitalization'. I raised my eyebrows thinking that this was just a buzz word that they felt compelled to drag out, but then they explained what they meant. Pipes aren't just pipes anymore. They are pieces of technological wizardry, infused with sensors to measure flow, temperature, pressure, acidity... and communications technology to relay the data back to the control centre.

Pipe companies that simply supply pipes are so last millennium! If pipes need to be connected to the web, what next?

The benefits of IOT technology in business are obvious – the ability to spot problems before they happen, planning upgrades and enhancements ahead of time, preventative maintenance, accurate diagnosis, efficiency gains, making our lives better and easier.

The benefits in the home are sometimes less obvious, but that hasn't stopped us adopting the technology with gusto and unfettered optimism. High-definition home security systems that are controlled from your smart-phone are cheap and easy to install. A simple demonstration video doing the rounds on social media showed a delivery man ringing the doorbell of an empty home. The owner, answering the door via their smartphone from their desk at work, sees and speaks to the courier and explains that no-one is home. She then presses a button on her phone and opens the boot of the Tesla parked in the driveway and asks the delivery man to place the package in the boot of her car. He does so, she closes the boot, locks the car and the courier gets on with the rest of his day, slightly bemused.

Of course, every silver lining has a cloud. Take Amazon's Alexa, which lets us access the internet and control the things we have connected to it with our voices – a boon to the elderly and sofa-surfers alike! But to do this, it must listen to everything we say and do. In 2018, Alexa started laughing at random times in thousands of houses across the world. No-one is quite sure why. Your iPhone's Siri does this too. (Listens, not laughs.) In fact, rumours abound that your Facebook feed will show you ads based upon what your iPhone has overheard, even if Facebook isn't open. Facebook has strenuously denied this, but many remain unconvinced. The web is full of people describing how soon after they had been talking of getting a cat, they are presented with ads for cat food or of talking about needing an iPhone accessory and then receiving an ad for them only minutes later. These events could be coincidence and a heightened awareness of the subject matter you have been discussing, but could a company like Facebook listen in to your conversations? Technically, yes they could. Yes they can.

Security is another big risk when it comes to IOT. Now they are connected, your lights, heating, fridge, even your waste pipes (?) could all be hacked into and controlled by someone else. Cyber hackers could control every aspect of our lives – and the fact that all of this technology has been adopted so rapidly means that the whole shambolic network has been designed for users with little regard for how to keep it all secure. Disrupting conversations between your kettle and your TV is one thing. Disrupting communications between your office building and its security firm is quite another.

Why build when you can print?

What do human ears, model aeroplanes, car components, running shoes, pizza, guns, musical instruments, clothes, furniture and houses have in common? They can all be made using 3-D printing.

The applications for this technology appear to be endless. We can even print houses! Real, live houses. This feat was heralded back in 2016, when His Highness Sheikh Mohammad Bin Rashid Al Maktoum, Vice-President and Prime Minister of the UAE and Ruler of Dubai unveiled the world's first fully functional 3-D printed house. Only a few years later, the price of 3-D printing small houses or apartments has shrunk to as low as US $10,000.

This technology has the potential to streamline manufacturing and design processes across a plethora of industries, reduce costs and create a slew of new jobs in disciplines that we are yet to even categorize properly. In doing this, 3-D printing will follow the time-honoured tradition of new technologies and render many existing manufacturing jobs superfluous to requirements while creating brand new jobs in other parts of the economy.

3-D printing will render many existing manufacturing jobs superfluous to requirements while creating brand new jobs in other parts of the economy.

Artificial intelligence: terminator or liberator?

Artificial intelligence (AI) is all the rage. The arrival of machines that can learn and adapt was announced loudly and clearly in 2016 when Google's 'Deep Mind' program beat the Go world champion – a game that we thought was too complex and subtle for a computer to ever triumph over a human. We were wrong.

IBM's Artificial Intelligence Unit, IBM Watson, is now powering a host of exciting new AI developments – including life-like customer service avatars that spell the beginning of the end for human call centres. These avatars are a product of a New Zealand company called Soul Machines (www.soulmachines.com), can deliver the sort of customer experience that you would expect from the best human customer service agent on his/her best day – and yet Rachel can provide this simultaneously to many thousands of people 24 hours a day, 7 days a week. She uses our laptop's microphone and camera to note and react to our emotional reactions and she gets better with every interaction. We used to outsource our call centres to India, Indonesia, The Philippines or Scotland. Soon, very soon, we will be outsourcing them to The Cloud. I predict this will start to happen within 10's and 20's of months, not 10's and 20's of years.

Soul Machine's customer service avatars are just the tip of the AI iceberg. As of 2018, Microsoft employed 5,000 AI professionals in China alone. 'Google Brain' is based in Mountain View, California, and has satellite groups in Cambridge (Massachusetts), London, Montreal, New York City, San Francisco, Toronto and Zurich – all staffed with master's and PhD graduates focusing their collaborative efforts on AI.

At the M&A Advisor Summit in New York in November 2017, at which I was invited to speak about change, Dr Kai Fu Lee, Chinese academic, AI expert, government adviser and best-selling author on the subject described four waves of AI:

1 *The internet data wave*: This is the current wave dominated by the large internet companies that use and control the immense amount of data that we willingly hand over to them so that they can tailor our online shopping and viewing experiences. They use simple AI algorithms to show us news, 'fake news' and advertising we will like. Google, Amazon, Facebook, Alibaba and WeChat are the current winners. But it is still early days when it comes to AI.

2 *New data AI*: Pattern recognition. Facial recognition. This wave has also begun. It will see the merger of offline and online capability. For example, face recognition software will recognize us from our online profile the moment we step into a physical store. Airport passport gates are already using an early version of this capability. Pattern recognition software can already detect cancers better than the best oncologists (see later).

3 *Mechanical AI*: This wave will see clever machine learning algorithms control physical things. Driverless cars fit into this category.

4 *Full automation*: The world when robots are so sophisticated that they can do manual work better than humans.

In October 2019, Google announced it had taken AI one incredible step further with a Quantum Computer that could perform an incredibly complex calculation in a number of seconds that an 'ordinary' super computer would take thousands of years to complete. The human brain may have just been surpassed.

Ray Kurzweil, ex-Google, a director of The Singularity University and winner of the 1999 US National Medal of Technology and Innovation, predicted that, by 2029, 'the manufacturing, agriculture, and transportation sectors of the economy will be almost entirely automated'.[3]

I think he may have been too conservative as the disruption won't only be confined to those three industries. Every industry will be disrupted by AI and advanced automation. In the not-too-distant-future, we will need far fewer lawyers, accountants, financial advisers, bankers, investment professionals... every industry's employment model will be turned on its head.

The removal of humans from factories has been happening for decades, devastating traditional manufacturing communities in the process – and no matter what promises are made by politicians, those jobs aren't coming back. If Mexican factories were forced to return to Detroit, they would be heavily automated. With US workers costing five times as much as Mexican workers, factory owners would have no choice but to automate. Even Carrier Air-Conditioning, which became the poster-child for 'bringing jobs back to America' before and after the 2016 US Presidential election, had plans to automate their workforce – most likely with the help of the US $7 million tax break that Vice President Pence secured from the taxpayers of Indiana.[4] 'We're going to automate to drive the cost down so that we can continue to be competitive', he said. 'What that ultimately means is there will be fewer jobs.'

In the not-too-distant-future, we will need far fewer lawyers, accountants, financial advisers, bankers, investment professionals.

Ironically, given that cheap workers have been at the heart of the Chinese economic miracle, China is leading the way with advanced robotics. According to Seattle-based Allen Institute for Artificial Intelligence, China has overtaken the United States in terms of both the quantity and quality of AI research.

Back in 2014, China's President Xi Jinping called for a 'robot revolution'. 'China wants to replace millions of workers with robots' announced the MIT Technology Review a year later. In 2016, the FT gave us a glimpse of China's 'Robot Revolution' in an article about a sink manufacturer, Ying Ao, that made 1,500 sinks a day. Due to reasons that the article didn't go into in great detail, Ying Ao's owner was forced to pay his staff US $1,200 a month, twice the average rate of pay in the rest of the Guangdong Province. This spurred him on to replace 140 of his people with just nine robots. 'These machines are cheaper, more precise and more reliable than people', the owner declared to the FT. 'I've never had a whole batch ruined by robots. I look forward to replacing more humans in future.' If a US $1,200 per month worker in China can be replaced by robots, workers in the West are in real trouble.

If a US $1,200 per month worker in China can be replaced by robots, workers in the West are in real trouble.

But it isn't only factory jobs that are at risk. Dr Lee believes that as many as 50 per cent of today's 'white collar' jobs will be done by machines by 2030.

In the UK, Brexit is unlikely to improve the situation. Foreign firms will now pause to question future investment in the UK now that it is no longer part of the six-times-larger European Union. In fact it is already happening. Late in 2019, Tesla chose Germany over the UK for its new electric car factory, citing Brexit as a key reason. The list of firms that have already removed jobs, moved jobs or moved offices out of the UK because of Brexit as of writing this chapter includes Airbus, Aviva, Credit Suisse, Jaguar Land Rover, HSBC, Goldman Sachs, Panasonic, Sony, Nomura, Daiwa, Norinchukin Bank, WebTrade, Lloyds of London, Hermes Investment Management, Panasonic, P&O, Philips, Unilever, JPMorgan, Barclays, Bank of America, UBS, Moneygram, Total... even firms such as Dyson run by arch-Brexiteers have upped sticks.

While a number of small-medium exporters are likely to struggle, unable to unravel their EU supply chains or find enough qualified or willing staff, new business opportunities will emerge from the chaos. I look forward to seeing what they are.

Those businesses that remain in the UK will automate as much as possible. Actually, so will many of those that move to Europe, come to think of it. The good news is that new jobs will be created as old jobs are lost.

A 2017 article in *Forbes* magazine declared that while 7 million US manufacturing jobs had disappeared since its 1979 peak, 53 million non-manufacturing jobs had been created and that 33 million of these were in higher paying jobs. Where was this statistic during the 2016 Presidential election?! The OECD is a little more conservative and simply reports that considerably more jobs have been created in high-tech industries and services within OECD countries than the number that have been lost in traditional manufacturing as a result of globalization and the internet. Yet, try telling that to people who have lost their livelihoods in the 'rust belt' of the United States, the UK's traditional manufacturing heartlands, or the swathes of people who have been losing their jobs in a rapidly shrinking bricks-and-mortar retail sector across the West.

So, while intelligent machines and programmes may indeed replace significant numbers of human jobs in the not-too-distant future, other jobs will emerge – and if globalization is anything to go by, the numbers of new jobs created may even be greater than the numbers of traditional jobs that have been lost. In fact, the World Economic Forum believes that AI will create twice as many jobs as it destroys.

However, as we saw with globalization, these jobs will require different skills and will probably be located in different parts of the country. We will all have to learn, unlearn and re-learn many times in our careers. And we have learnt from globalization that assistance from government or our employers is likely to be patchy and inadequate.

It will be up to each one of us to make the transition ourselves.

Augmented intelligence

AI may not be something to fear. Embracing it may indeed be the best solution – for AI also stands for 'Augmented Intelligence'. The blending of humans and self-learning intelligent software programs and machines will help us to do our jobs even better.

Oncologists are a brilliant case in point. When it was announced that pattern-recognition software could detect cancers in X-rays better than a panel of the best oncologists, some people started to fear for the future of the oncology profession. This fear was unfounded. The software helps oncologists to focus on cells that they may have overlooked. They now miss far fewer cancers and detect them much earlier, enabling them to get on with saving more lives than ever before, further aided by computer-guided lasers and scalpels if required.

AI professionals across the globe are striving to create computers with the intelligence to form their own insights. Computers can sift through mountains of data far quicker than we can and then provide us with the ability to make sense of it all. Anaplan (www.anaplan.com) does precisely this. Their clever algorithms enable executives to make more informed decisions. They sift through terabytes of data and turn it into knowledge. The executives are then able to turn this knowledge into insight and action. Anaplan's clever algorithms don't replace executives; they enhance their performance.

But computers cannot do it alone. On a train to Paris in 2017, I sat next to a brilliant young woman with a PhD in Linguistics who was about to jet off to San Francisco to train Google's Assistant to better understand human speech, tone and emotion as it is portrayed through voice. This is a job that could hardly have been dreamt of even a few short years ago.

I believe that AI will prove to be more useful as an extension to, rather than a replacement for, human intelligence. We may even be able to harness the power of computing to make ourselves more intelligent. Anyone who has worked in a fully functional team will have experienced the synergistic effect of several brains working together. More and more, our teams will include computers.

Cars are so last millennium

If the doyens of Silicon Valley are to be believed, it may take less than a decade for our city streets to be bumper-to-bumper with electric cars and no drivers. I wouldn't be surprised if Singapore were the first city to go completely driverless. It is estimated that there are 1.3 billion cars on the planet with an additional 94 million being constructed every year. These vehicles are idle 90 per cent of the time. After the driverless car revolution, the total car market could shrink, some say to as little as 100 million vehicles globally. Talk about an industry that will change!

The companies leading the driverless car revolution are not just the traditional car manufacturers such as Toyota, Ford, VW, BMW and Fiat Chrysler but also include the likes of Google, Apple, Tesla, Intel and Bosch plus tech firms that few of us would recognize – Baidu, Nutonomy, Mobileye, Nvidia and FiveAI. Intel bought Israel-based Mobileye for US $15 billion.

The auto industry and the tech industry are merging. And so will the auto industry, commercial real estate and hospitality industries. When a car no longer has a driver, it can be much more than a car. It can be a driverless hotel room, a driverless meeting room, a driverless office, a driverless cinema or shop or gym... When you next arrive at an airport, it may not be a taxi that meets you; it could be your driverless hotel room that sweeps you up and takes you to where you are staying the night.

Science fiction becomes science fact. On 9 January 2018, Toyota launched a dedicated mobility services vehicle and announced it would become a driverless room manufacturer using their e-Palette drivetrain, as it transforms itself into a 'mobility service company'.

All change!

CHAPTER TWO

The age of the centurian

Ask what your 20-year-old self would think of you today.
We invite you to think about what your 70, 80 or 100-year-old
self would think of you now. LYNDA GRATTON[1]

In 1900, the average worldwide life expectancy at birth was just 31 years.[2] Life expectancy for a white male in the United States back in 1900 was 47 and just 33 for a US male of African descent.[3] Today, that gap at least has closed almost entirely to 77 and 76 respectively.[4]

In 2017, the worldwide average life expectancy was 81, ranging from 84 in Hong Kong, Japan, Singapore and Italy, 83 in the likes of Switzerland, Australia, Iceland, France, Canada and South Korea, 82 in the rest of mainland Europe, 81 in the UK, 80 in Cuba, 79.5 in the United States and as low as 49 to 59 throughout much of Africa.[5] The proportion of Americans who reach the age of 65 has tripled since 1900, from 30 to 90 per cent.[6] Five per cent of British males now live to 96 (98 for females).[7]

Dr Lee, whom I quoted in Chapter 1, predicts that our life expectancy could rise by a year for every year of the 2030s. If he is right, by 2027, our average life expectancy could be well into the 90s. A baby born in the West today has a 50 per cent chance of living until 100.

But it is oh so much better to be rich. Life expectancy can vary by 20 years or more depending on where you live in the United States, according to a 2017 study by the University of Washington.[8]

We humans no longer die in such large numbers from droughts, floods, crop failures or famine. In fact, three times as many humans die from over-eating than from malnutrition.[9]

Three times as many humans die from over-eating than from malnutrition.

We also don't seem to succumb to disease in the way our ancestors did thanks to immunization, anti-biotics and the fact that our world is far better organized. Every outbreak of new and dangerous diseases, so far, has been contained – AIDS, bird flu, SARS, MERS, Ebola, hopefully even COVID-19...

A logical way to increase human lifespans even further would be to wean the West off its addiction to sugar, for this sweet poison seems to have taken the place of famine and disease. More people die today from diabetes and sugar-fuelled cancers than war, crime, terrorism or suicide.[10] As Yuval Noah Harari phrased it in his excellent book *Homo Deus*, 'sugar is now more dangerous than gunpowder'. If you wish to explore this subject further, two brilliant movies I recommend are *Fed Up* from the United States and *That Sugar Film* from Australia. Another excellent film on this subject is *Forks over Knives*, which explores how an organic, vegetarian diet can reverse diabetes and even shrink certain cancerous tumours.

But while removing excess sugar from our diets will almost certainly help us to live longer, if we wish to achieve a quantum leap in longevity we will need to turn to the laboratory. New treatments now use our own body's immune system to fight cancer. The ability to grow our own organs in laboratories is moving beyond the theoretical. Stem cells may even be used to revitalize old cells and slow the ageing process.

Could ageing, one day, be stopped altogether?

Who wants to live forever?

What if death were viewed as a technical challenge rather than a biological certainty?

Back in 2013, Google launched a company with precisely this point of view. The Californian Life Company, or Calico, was launched with the incredible aim of 'solving death'. Calico describes itself as:

> A research and development company whose mission is to harness advanced technologies to increase our understanding of the biology that controls lifespan. We will use that knowledge to devise interventions that enable people to lead longer and healthier lives.[11]

Has the first person who could live to 300 already been born?

CHAPTER THREE

Climate change

The dangerous power of denial

In the beautiful Midwest, wind chill temperatures are reaching minus 60 degrees, the coldest ever recorded. In coming days, expected to get even colder. People can't last outside even for minutes. What the hell is going on with Global Warming? Please come back fast, we need you!

DONALD TRUMP, PRESIDENT OF THE UNITED STATES AND ARCH CLIMATE CHANGE DENIER VIA TWITTER (OBVIOUSLY), 29 JANUARY 2019

Climate change has become a battleground. It is not only a battle between man and nature; it is also a battle between science and dogma; between scientists who deal in probabilities and the majority of us who mistake probabilities for guesswork.

Never before has science been so mistrusted. Never before have the motives of scientists been brought into question in such a public, partisan and emotional manner.

The reason is hope and fear. Hope that the scientists are wrong and fear that if we were to drastically reduce our production of greenhouse gases to the degree that the scientists are recommending, it would significantly and negatively affect our economies and our standards of living. And the fear is understandable. Today's global economy is run on fossil fuels, livestock and, to a lesser extent, palm oil – each of which is adversely affecting the planet as we know it in dramatic and life-changing ways.

But the scientific community is clear: human activity is warming our planet to such an extent that devastating changes may soon become irreversible.

And yet significant numbers of people simply don't believe the science – or don't want to believe it. They are egged on by a small but increasing number of populist politicians who are vocal climate science sceptics or outright deniers, who are playing on and amplifying the understandable concerns of the electorate.

Human activity is warming our planet to such an extent that devastating changes may soon become irreversible.

Climate change scepticism may be understandable, but it is not logical. Because no matter which side of the argument we tend towards, we can all agree on three key irrefutable facts:

1 *The greenhouse effect is real*: Solar energy absorbed at the Earth's surface is radiated back into the atmosphere as heat. As the heat makes its way through the atmosphere and back out to space, greenhouse gases absorb much of it, thus keeping the planet 'warm'. Without it, most of the Earth would be a frozen wasteland and we probably wouldn't even exist.

2 *Global CO_2 levels in our atmosphere have increased dramatically since the industrial revolution*: Levels have been accelerating at an alarming rate during the last century. According to NASA, the CO_2 in our atmosphere has fluctuated between 180 parts per million (ppm) and 290 ppm for the last 400,000 years. In the last 100 years, the concentration of CO_2 in our atmosphere has shot up to more than 409 ppm and it is still rising. NASA's graph of this shows a vertical line that shows no signs of stopping its relentless ascent. CO_2, along with methane, is an incredibly powerful greenhouse gas.

3 *This dramatic increase in CO_2 levels has coincided with a 10-fold increase in human-produced CO_2 emissions during the same period.*

Yet many populist politicians and sceptics dispute that there may be any link between #3 and #2; that the dramatic increase in human-produced CO_2 is the cause of the dramatic rise in CO_2 levels in the atmosphere.

I find this baffling, because the science is clear…

The US Met Office has reported that sea temperatures have risen about 1°C since pre-industrial times.

The warmest year on record that did not receive a temperature boost from El Niño was 2017.[1] The cause, according to the American Meteorological Society, was because 'the dominant greenhouse gases released into Earth's atmosphere – carbon dioxide, methane and nitrous oxide – increased once again in 2017, reaching new record highs'.

And 2018 was even hotter. As meteorological offices around the world have reported, the 20 hottest years on record have been in the last 22 years.

Then 2019 was even hotter again. It looks like the 2010s were the hottest decade on record.

Rising sea levels

The Intergovernmental Panel on Climate Change (IPCC) concurs with NASA and the Met Office. Its 2014 report concluded that man-made greenhouse gas emissions are now at levels that 'are unprecedented in at least the last 800,000 years. Their effects are extremely likely to have been the dominant cause of the observed warming since the mid-20th century'. It also concluded that the oceans 'will continue to warm and acidify, and global mean sea level to rise (between 0.3 m – 1 m by 2100 depending upon the scenario)'.

But, if sea levels are rising as the IPCC claims, why aren't the Maldives under water? Because the rise in sea levels is *accelerating*. The IPCC's prediction is based on a logical extrapolation of the growth in sea levels that we have seen since 1900. What many of us, myself included, have failed to grasp is that the rise in sea levels hasn't been linear – it has been exponential.

The global sea level is 5 to 8 inches (13 to 20 cm) higher on average than it was in 1900, according to the Smithsonian Institute.[2] That has been hardly noticeable and certainly not enough to turn Malé into Atlantis.

The critical point is that half of this rise has occurred since the mid-1900s.[3] Throughout most of the 20th century, the sea level rose between 1.2 and 1.7 mm per year on average. Today the rate is double that – around 3.4 mm per year.

If the growth continues to accelerate (which is the logical assumption), we will witness an average sea level rise of an additional 15 to 20 cm by the mid-2040s and a further rise of an extra 30 to 40 cm during the 25 years after that. The average sea level in 2070 would then be 45 to 60 cm (up to two feet) higher than today (and 60 to 80 cm higher than it was in 1900).

This would be catastrophic – and it is the trajectory we are currently on.

All of these reports should be game-changers. Unfortunately, there are simply too many vested interests promoting the business of climate change denial.

When opinions trump facts

A vocal minority, including the 45th President of the United States, seem to dismiss the very concept of man-made climate change as a 'triumph of the greenies, bureaucrats and liberal elites'; as 'political correctness gone mad'. It is part of a dangerous and growing disdain across the West for the opinions of experts that opportunistic politicians have seized upon to dismiss the considered evidence-based conclusions of many hundreds of scientists from all continents as 'scaremongering'.

We live in a strange world where baseless opinions seem to hold as much credibility as facts, sometimes more. In 2012, Donald Trump tweeted: 'The concept of global warming was created by and for the Chinese in order to make U.S. manufacturing non-competitive' and his baseless comments weren't shot down in flames; they were either laughed at or ignored – by everyone except for his ardent and loyal supporter base.

We live in a strange world where baseless opinions seem to hold as much credibility as facts, sometimes more.

Six years later, in a *60 minutes* interview, he altered his stance a little: 'I think something's happening. Something's changing and it'll change back again', he proclaimed, offering no evidence to support the second part of that last sentence. He then continued: 'I don't think it's a hoax. I think there's probably a difference. But I don't know that it's man-made. I will say this: I don't want to give away trillions and trillions of dollars. I don't want to lose millions and millions of jobs'.

And there's the rub. It's about money. It's about jobs. What he is really saying is that it is about short-term money and short-term jobs. But he is not only wrong; he is also doing the wrong thing by his people. He is forgoing massive economic opportunities by living in the past.

The United States is the largest historical producer of greenhouse gases, and even though China now produces more per annum, the United States is by far the largest producer of greenhouse gases per capita. Furthermore, we in the West effectively 'outsource' our manufacturing emissions to China with every product we import.

Not only has the latest US President rolled back countless environmental programmes instigated by his predecessor, but perhaps worst of all he has pulled the United States out of the Paris Climate Agreement.

The Paris accord was signed by nearly 200 countries in December 2015 in an effort to create a more effective international response to curb greenhouse gas emissions with the ultimate ambition of limiting global warming to 2˚C. The United States is now the only country in the world not to be a signatory to the agreement.

Trumping the President

Fortunately, state governors are stepping into the leadership void created by the Trump administration.

'While the White House declares war on climate science and retreats from the Paris Agreement, California is doing the opposite and taking action', said California Governor Jerry Brown.

'Reducing CO_2 emissions by improving energy efficiency and increasing renewable energy have helped Oregon achieve the fastest job growth rate in the US', declared Oregon Governor Kate Brown.

'More than 57,000 clean energy jobs have been created recently in Minnesota', said Stephanie Zawistowski, a senior policy adviser to Governor Mark Dayton.

Oregon, California and Minnesota are part of the bipartisan United States Climate Alliance, which is composed of 15 states and territories, representing 116 million Americans. All have committed to meet or beat the targets of the Paris Agreement. New York State has cut emissions from the power sector by nearly 50 per cent since 1990 and plans to stop using coal this year.

But this isn't only confined to the United States. Some 94 of the world's major cities (and growing) around the world are bypassing their often recalcitrant national governments to tackle climate change together. 'C40 Cities' (c40.org) helps its member cities to 'take bold climate action, leading the way towards a healthier and more sustainable future'. The cities include New York, Boston, Philadelphia, Los Angeles, London, Paris, Madrid, Barcelona, Lisbon, Addis Ababa, Nairobi, Lagos, Capetown, Johannesburg, Hong Kong, Saigon, Singapore, Sydney, Melbourne, Auckland… and they represent more than 700 million residents and a quarter of the global economy.

A separate organization, The Global Covenant of Mayors, is a similar global alliance of over 10,000 cities and local governments from 6 continents and 138 countries. ICLEI is a worldwide community of 1,750 local and regional governments promoting and enabling sustainable, low-emission urban development. UK100 (uk100.org) is a network of local government leaders who have pledged to shift to 100 per cent clean energy by 2050.

When it comes to climate change, many national governments are very slow or unwilling to act. Luckily, across the world, regional, local and city governors are stepping up to the plate. They know that ignoring climate change is likely to cost billions. They also know that climate-change-denying economies will miss out on future waves of jobs creation in exciting new industries. Embracing climate science opens up new opportunities in tomorrow's low-carbon economy.

It's not about going back to the Dark Ages; it's about embracing the future.

CHAPTER FOUR

Boyan Slat and the Millennials

Pessimism is what preserves the status quo.
Optimism is what propels us forward. BOYAN SLAT[1]

Drowning in plastic

Over 5 trillion pieces of plastic litter our oceans.[2] And it's only getting worse.

Some 8 to 12 million tonnes of plastic find their way into our oceans every year, according to Dr Jenna Jambeck of the University of Georgia.[3] Europe's Danube River alone releases approximately 1,700 tonnes of plastic into the sea annually.[4] On just one day in 2014, International Coastal Cleanup volunteers collected more than 5,500 tonnes of rubbish from our beaches. Some 500 billion plastic bags are used every year, and 100 billion plastic bottles were sold last year in the United States alone.

Scientists at Ghent University in Belgium have calculated that shellfish lovers are eating up to 11,000 plastic fragments in their seafood each year. We absorb less than 1 per cent of the plastic, but it will still accumulate in the body over time. A study by Plymouth University reported that plastic was found in a third of UK-caught fish.[5]

Transported by ocean currents, all this plastic ends up amassing in enormous clumps in our oceans. There's even a 'little' one in the Mediterranean Sea. The

Mediterranean Garbage Patch contains 250 billion pieces of plastic making up 500 tonnes of rubbish. But this pales into insignificance when compared to The Great Atlantic Garbage Patch, The Indian Ocean Garbage Patch and Grand-Daddy of them all, The Great Pacific Garbage Patch located between California and Hawaii. This last one is estimated to contain up to 3.6 trillion pieces of plastic and weigh in at 100,000 tonnes across an area that is estimated to cover 1.6 million square kilometres, an area twice the size of Texas or three times the size of France (seven times the size of the UK).[6] The surface waters of the Great Pacific Garbage Patch contain 180 times more plastic than marine life by weight. Just read those figures again. What the hell are we doing to our oceans?

To the rescue has come an amazing 18-year-old. In February 2013, a Norwegian teenager by the name of Boyan Slat dropped out of his Aerospace Engineering studies at TU Delft to start The Ocean Cleanup (www.theoceancleanup.com) with the aim of cleaning up 50 per cent of the Great Pacific Garbage Patch within five years. His first prototype was deployed in June 2016, and The Ocean Cleanup launched the first full-scale operational system into the Great Pacific Garbage Patch in September 2018.

They have developed a passive system, moving with the currents, just like the plastic, to collect it. The Ocean Cleanup's system is composed of a floater with a solid screen underneath, concentrating the debris and leading it to a collection system. The system is slowed down by a drift anchor suspended at an approximate depth of 600 metres, making the system move slower than the plastic and therefore catching it. They plan to convert the lower quality plastics into diesel fuel and recycle the higher quality plastic to help fund the cleanup project.

Boyan Slat is the youngest ever recipient of the UN's highest environmental accolade: Champion of the Earth. In 2015, HM King Harald of Norway awarded Boyan the maritime industry's Young Entrepreneur Award. *Foreign Policy* included Boyan in their 2015 list of pre-eminent thought leaders, *Forbes* included him in their 30 under 30 edition in 2016, and *Reader's Digest* chose him as the European of the Year in 2017. That year he was also given the Thor Heyerdahl award and was named one of the 100 world's most intriguing entrepreneurs by Goldman Sachs. Boyan is a member of the Thiel Fellowship. The Ocean Cleanup was chosen by *TIME* magazine as one of the 25 best inventions of 2015.

Boyan's determination and drive may hopefully spur on governments across the world to invest in robust recycling technologies, industries and manufacturers to get rid of the tonnes and tonnes of unnecessary plastic that our food and goods come wrapped in. Big changes need to happen.

The Millennials

Boyan Slat is one of the most impressive of his generation: the Millennials. I love the Millennials. This generation is now in their twenties and early thirties and starting to impact the world they have inherited. Their parents' generation is more prosperous than they collectively may ever be, and the Millennials will have to wait until they are well past 60 before they inherit anything at all due to the fact their parents are living so much longer – if there is much left to inherit after the costs of aged care. Furthermore, the previous generation is staying at work longer. Some 22 per cent of the US workforce is aged 55 or over, up from just 12 per cent 20 years ago. This figure is forecast to increase to 25 per cent by 2024.

Even with all of this going against them, the Millennials are idealistic. They have a sense of purpose. When my generation left school, we wanted to make a living. This generation wants to make a difference. And they mean it. They won't join companies who don't take corporate social responsibility or sustainability seriously, and they will leave organizations if they discover that the executives aren't genuinely living up to the corporate values that are printed in the annual reports. They work hard and they are dedicated, but they also demand work–life balance from the get-go. Several of my generation regard them as entitled and lazy because they don't want to work 60 hours a week or pull all-nighters for a client.

If we can just let go of the reins, the Millennials may just save the world.

They are wrong. 'They will work hard, just not for your crappy job' is an article that succinctly explains why.[7]

My generation and the one before us made the world a more prosperous place. The last two generations have pulled hundreds of millions, if not billions, of people out of poverty. But we have also created an immoral and highly dangerous inequality gap. In 1965, the average CEO of a US listed

31

company earned 20 times as much as (his) average worker. Today the ratio exceeds 300[8] – a CEO can earn as much in a day as many of their workers earn in a year. Wealth inequality is equally as wide. The top 0.1 per cent owns as much as the 'bottom' 90 per cent of the population.

And, as Boyan may have noticed, we have stuffed the planet up royally. We are passing to the Millennials a world full of scientific marvels and opportunities but also a world of untold risks and serious problems. I have utmost faith in the next generation. If we can just let go of the reins of this precious planet, the Millennials may just save the world.

CHAPTER FIVE

The way we work has changed forever

The most important skill for humans in the 21st century will be the ability to reinvent ourselves – because of the rapid pace of technological change, especially in the job market. YUVAL NOAH HARARI[1]

The 'job for life' is long gone. The 'career for life' days are also over. Not that long ago, your CV needed to show stability; the fewer employers the better. Today, that would signify a lack of initiative, perhaps even a lack of talent.

Under-employment is on the rise. Our nations' historically low unemployment figures hide drastic under-employment figures. In the UK, Australia and the United States, if you work just one hour of paid work, you are classified as 'employed'. According to a pre-COVID survey of 900,000 people by Payscale.com, 46 per cent of US workers believed they were under-employed. Gallup calculate the figure to be 14.1 per cent, still much higher than the pre-COVID c. 4 per cent official unemployment rate at the time.

Self-employment is also on the rise. Ten per cent of Americans are self-employed. More than one in seven British people are self-employed. Forty years ago this ratio was 1 in 11. There are now 5 million self-employed people in the UK out of 32 million people in work. Almost 9 million (27 per cent) are employed part-time.[2]

If you lean to the right politically, you will deduce that this boom in self-employment has 'helped drive a recovery in employment', which has risen from 70 per cent in 2011 to a record high of 76 per cent in 2018.[3]

If you lean to the left, you will regard the rise in self-employment to be 'driving lower pay and retirement income and eroding job security and tax revenue'.[4] Obviously, not all self-employed are successful entrepreneurs! Many are on zero-hour contracts, unsure when the next pay cheque will come in or how large it will be. The UK's Office of National Statistics reports that fewer people left self-employment over the last five years than at any period in the last 20 years, suggesting that they have struggled to find an alternative job during the prolonged economic malaise.

Increasingly, under-employment and self-employment go hand in hand.

Self-employed, anxious and earning low wages: welcome to the gig economy

The 'gig economy', led by the likes of Uber and Airbnb, is coming under global scrutiny. What started out as the 'shared economy', where people could rent out a spare room or use their car as an occasional taxi, has quickly morphed into businesses that seem to be taking advantage of the weak negotiating position of their 'employees'. 'But our drivers really value the flexible working hours' is true (see below), but it belies the fact that many Uber drivers don't really have a choice. Many of them I would define as 'working poor' – without security of tenure, minimum pay, benefits or rights.

Eighty per cent of London Uber drivers say that they prefer flexible over fixed hours. According to a 2018 study by Oxford University, 82 per cent of London's Uber drivers 'strongly agree' with the statement 'Being able to choose my own hours is more important than having holiday pay and a guaranteed minimum wage', and 84 per cent say, 'I don't want to work for a traditional company in case I lose the flexibility I have'. Some 93 per cent agree with the statement, 'I partnered with Uber to have more flexibility in my schedule and balance my work life and family'. Almost every driver was employed before joining Uber and while almost half of them said their income had increased since joining, three-quarters of Uber drivers reported a lower income than the median London gross weekly pay.

With Uber, they are less poor than they used to be. They are also more anxious. As Dr Berger, Associate Fellow of the Oxford Martin Programme on Technology and Employment, explained: 'Uber drivers reported that they suffered more anxiety than those in waged employment, a finding consistent with previous studies showing self-employed workers are more satisfied with their lives, but also experience more negative emotions'.

On Friday 10 May 2019, Uber listed on the New York Stock Exchange at a valuation of US $76.5 billion, enriching its shareholders and executives to an unfathomable extent. At the same time, Uber drivers were striking in capital cities worldwide about their low pay and utter lack of protection.

Uber is the poster child for Irresponsible Capitalism: a business with no realistic plan to ever make a profit (it currently loses c. US $3 billion a year) that provides cheap taxi services globally by exploiting the 'working poor' while transforming a handful of people into billionaires. (And yet the service it provides is fantastic!)

The lows of the High Street

Amazon is killing traditional retail. Main Streets and High Streets across the West are losing one shop after another as we all do so much more of our shopping online. Out-of-town malls, once the darling of investors across the world, are dying too. Banks continue to close branches as we hardly use them anymore. The only thing I have used a bank branch for in the last decade is to deposit the odd cheque. Now my banking app even enables me to scan the cheque using my phone's camera and it is instantly deposited into my account. Branches are becoming redundant – along with the people who used to work in them.

The High Street will evolve. Main Streets will become places for social interaction, not just shopping. Places we go to eat, drink and socialize while the supermarket's robots pick our shopping and Amazon's drones deliver everything else.

Employer loyalty continues to wane

To many companies, we are simply resources – 'human resources'. Redundancy is a normal experience, one that we will experience several times in our careers. Even though each time it feels like a blow to the solar plexus, we simply have to cope with it.

Employer and employee loyalty are becoming concepts from a bygone era.

Employer and employee loyalty are also becoming concepts from a bygone era. The latest generation understands this completely.

In the future, even more of us will be self-employed. We will be changing jobs frequently and we will be juggling several employers/clients at the one time.

A senior partner of one of the world's largest global consultancy firms told me that the future model for his firm was 'A core group of (far fewer) employees employing large numbers of contractors as required'. Our jobs, our careers, our skills development, our livelihoods are all in our hands.

We have no choice but to embrace the change.

Embrace the change

We have only scratched the surface with all of the topics covered in Part One.

We haven't even mentioned a myriad of major tech advancements such as genetic modification (GM) or genetic engineering (GE), both of which, like Donald Trump, Brexit and Marmite, divide people into two completely opposite and unassailable camps. GM and GE are either utterly evil or the saviour of the human race. Genetic modification of crops produces disease-resistant strains of wheat that could be used to feed the world, yet we also fear the unknown consequences of tampering with nature in such a fundamental fashion. But it isn't only plants that we are tampering with. Scientists in China created fully functioning baby mice from the DNA of two female mice in 2018. Not one male mouse came anywhere near the process. Later that year, two twin girls, Lulu and Nan, became the world's first germline genome edited babies – an attempt to create HIV-resistant humans through

DNA modification. The biophysics researcher responsible for the experiment, He Jiankui, has since been jailed.

The biological and ethical implications of all this are a minefield. The future is shaping up to be like nothing that our species, our planet, our organizations and we have ever experienced. The way we live, the way we work, the way our organizations work, the way our governments work will all change, and the changes will be dramatic.

As I wrote in *The Change Catalyst:*[5]

Each of us has a simple choice:

1 **We can be ostriches**: shove our heads deep into the sand and pretend that change isn't happening. Or worse, convince ourselves that we can do nothing about it. Then, when the change inevitably arrives, we can then bask in our glorious victimhood or …

2 **We can be lionesses** (male lions are just lazy): meet the future head on, embrace the changes, find the opportunities and do our very best to reap the rewards of the new world.

The aim of this book is to help you channel your inner lioness.

PART TWO

The psychology of change

You have power over your mind, not outside events.
Realize this, and you will find strength. MARCUS AURELIUS[1]

Countless research projects have been undertaken by countless academics on the psychology of change and the findings can be broadly summed up as:

> We humans don't like change. In fact we are hard-wired to resist it. We erect
> barriers to change; we create obstacles that we put in our own way. Yet many
> of these obstacles are imaginary. They are the product of our own beliefs, biases
> and thoughts. They are the product of the stories we tell ourselves – about
> ourselves. We can overcome them.

The only way around these obstacles is first to realize they exist and then to realize that we have placed them there ourselves. Then, and only then, can we begin to devise some strategies and tactics to minimize them or navigate our way around them.

This book will help you to recognize the barriers you erect to change and it will help you work out ways to overcome those change barriers. Finally, it will help you plan for and embrace the future.

For the power to change lies within each of us.

It is, in a very real sense, all in the mind.

CHAPTER SIX

The power of the mind

The body achieves what the mind believes. ANONYMOUS

The human mind is an incredible thing – ethereal and yet at the same time very real. It is the most powerful tool we possess yet we are only beginning to understand its power. Our mind can make us feel physical pain when none actually exists. It can also reduce the effects of genuine physical pain, sometimes removing it altogether. Our mind can make us ill. It can make us well. It can make us depressed. It can make us anxious. It can make us happy. It can make us euphoric. It can make our heart race and temperature soar – with no physical causes whatsoever. We can also calm our pulse and cool our body – purely through the power of thought; the power of feeling; the power of the mind.

The placebo effect

One of the most incredible illustrations of the power of the mind is the placebo effect. 'Yes, I know about placeboes', I can hear you exclaim as your eyes roll heaven-wards. 'If we are given sugar pills but we think they are actual medicine then a significant percentage of us will genuinely feel better. Our minds will allow our body to heal itself.'

One of the most incredible illustrations of the power of the mind is the placebo effect.

But that isn't all. For some of us, even when we know there is absolutely nothing in the pills, we still get better! It is the act of taking the pill that somehow triggers the healing – even when we know there is no active ingredient whatsoever in the sham 'medicine' we are taking. As unbelievable as that may sound.

The *New Scientist* reported just such a case:

> Linda Buonanno had been sick with irritable bowel syndrome for 15 years when she saw a TV advertisement recruiting participants for a new study. Desperate for help, she signed on, even after learning that the potential treatments she would be offered consisted of either nothing – or pills filled with nothing. When the experiment ended, she begged the researchers to let her keep the pills. 'I felt fantastic', Buonanno said. 'I felt almost like I was before I got sick with IBS. It was the best three weeks of my life.' She has been trying to get her hands on more ever since.[1]

Imagine a future in which your doctor openly subscribes a placebo that enables your mind to heal your body. Imagine also a future when your doctor prescribes a series of meditation. For meditation can also have a similar effect. Not only does it boost our ability to think clearly, it also releases endorphins that provide a natural feeling of euphoria. Meditation can cause actual physical changes in the body.

Placebo surgery

Now let's imagine an even stranger world; one in which your doctor prescribes sham surgery! Yes placebo surgery is not only 'a thing', it has even been proven to work…

Back in 2002, the *New England Journal of Medicine* reported on a trial of 180 patients who were sent for arthroscopy of the knee for osteoarthritis. The patients were randomly assigned into three groups – two groups received different types of arthroscopic surgery. The third underwent 'placebo surgery'. Patients in the placebo group received skin incisions but without insertion of the arthroscope; nothing was done to their knees at all. Outcomes were assessed at multiple points over a 24-month period, including an objective test of walking and stair climbing. A total of 165 patients completed the trial.

The result? There was no 'clinically meaningful difference' between the placebo and either of the other groups. At no point did either of the intervention groups report less pain or better function than the placebo group. The outcomes of the patients who underwent actual surgery were no better than those who received the placebo procedure. Just think about that for a second or two.

Our mind can make us well.

It can also make us ill.

The nocebo effect

We can also suffer from a 'nocebo' effect, i.e. thinking we may have symptoms can actually bring them on. But not just symptoms, we can actually make ourselves physically sick purely through the power of the mind. Australian aborigines have known this for millennia. 'Pointing the bone' was an ancient tradition that would place a death curse on the recipient. If the recipient knew and believed, death was almost inevitable.

As Laird Hamilton, prolific big wave surfer and innovator says, 'Make sure your worst enemy doesn't live between your own two ears'.

Negative thoughts and beliefs can release cortisol, the 'stress hormone', which actually weakens our immune system. Too much cortisol 'can derail your body's most important functions. It can also lead to a number of health problems, including: Anxiety and depression, Headaches, Heart disease, Memory and concentration problems, Problems with digestion, Trouble sleeping, Weight gain'.[2]

Our negative thoughts can actually make us physically ill – and one estimate is that we may have tens of thousands of negative thoughts a day.

But our mind can also make us soar. For it gives us the power to imagine, to dream. Possibly unlike any other animal, we have the capacity to imagine things that haven't happened yet. This can be incredibly powerful. Pro golfers talk about visualizing the shot before hitting the ball. It's how successful entrepreneurs begin – imagining what success looks like is the first step towards striving to achieve it.

> *Nothing can stop the man with the right mental attitude*
> *from achieving his goal; nothing on earth can help the man*
> *with the wrong mental attitude.* THOMAS JEFFERSON[3]

CHAPTER SEVEN

All change is personal

All change is personal. All change is emotional. CAMPBELL MACPHERSON

Change comes in several forms – social change, political change, organizational change and personal change. But the common denominator across all of these different types of change is the last one: all change is personal.

The most complex organizational change is actually the amalgamation of hundreds and thousands of individual, personal changes. As I repeatedly remind business leaders, 'Only your people can deliver your strategy. Only your people can deliver the change the business requires'. If CEOs wish to be successful, they must invest time and energy into helping every one of their people through the process of change – at every single level of the organization starting with the members of the board and leadership team. The alternative is that the particular change, strategy, merger or acquisition will be one of the 88 per cent that fail to deliver the expected outcomes.

Change initiatives that fail, fail to engage properly with the people.

Change initiatives that fail, fail to engage properly with the people. And genuine engagement includes listening. It also requires treating every single person as the individual that they are – with individual motivations, aspirations and needs.

I also preach to CEOs that when it comes to change, emotions trump logic every time. Emotions rule our decisions. It doesn't matter how senior you are or how logical you may think you are, your decisions are ruled by your emotions. So, I advise leaders of change to work hard to find the emotional triggers for every one of their executives and managers, and to enable their managers to do the same for their people. I implore business leaders to invest in helping their people to make the necessary changes – for such investment will pay enormous dividends.

However, I have an even more important message for everyone who reads this book – you hold the keys to your own future.

If you want to change, you will have to do it yourself. There is no point waiting for someone else to do this for you – as the help may not arrive. You will need to help yourself make the transition. Your future is in your hands.

For it is not the size of the change that matters in the end, neither is it whether the change has been forced upon you. The all-important part of embracing change is how you react to it.

How you choose to react will make all the difference. And the choice is yours. You are in the driving seat. When change happens, how you react to it is entirely up to you.

All change is, indeed, personal.

CHAPTER EIGHT

All change is emotional

When dealing with people, remember you are not dealing with creatures of logic but creatures of emotion. DALE CARNEGIE[1]

Emotion trumps logic every time. This is especially true when it comes to change.

Every single decision we make is governed by our emotions. In fact, if we didn't have emotions, we wouldn't be able to make decisions at all.

Neuroscientist Professor Antonio Damasio[2] discovered this to be true after a study of people that had damaged the part of the brain where emotions are generated – or were born that way. They were like Spock of *Star Trek* – unable to feel emotions. Incredibly, they also couldn't make decisions! Even simple decisions such as what to eat or what to wear are impossible to make purely with logic. Decisions demand emotions. Professor Damasio's research shows that emotions play a central role in social cognition and decision-making. Not only do our emotions drive our decisions, we wouldn't be able to make decisions without them!

Emotion is four times more powerful than logic. A 2004 study of some 50,000 employees by the US-based Corporate Executive Council showed that, when it comes to engaging employees, emotional commitment is four times more powerful than rational commitment. Four times.

Successful marketers know this. Every successful ad campaign plays with our emotions – makes us laugh, cry, tugs at our heart strings, makes us angry, makes us jealous... Why else would they use a cute Labrador puppy to sell toilet tissue? Or foaming waves transforming into majestic white horses to sell Guinness?

Successful politicians also know the power of emotions all too well. All successful election campaigns play on our emotions – as was amply illustrated during the UK's 2016 EU referendum. David Cameron's calamitous campaign for Britain to remain in the EU completely ignored the fact that it is our emotions that drive our decision-making. Interestingly, the now ex-PM admitted this schoolboy error two years later while reflecting about the referendum in his opening address to a London conference at which I was also speaking.

Back in 2016, Cameron tried to convince people to vote 'Remain' through a mixture of logic, statistics, expert opinion and fear. What people needed was a positive emotional reason to vote for the EU – and none was forthcoming.

In direct contrast, the 'Leave' camp, with the opportunistic Boris Johnson as its front-man, appealed to the emotions of many millions of voters with a brilliant slogan, 'Vote Leave Take Back Control', a catchy 'Brexit' name and the promise of a better tomorrow outside of the EU. They played to an ingrained fear of foreigners among a significant minority of Britons (immigration was the primary reason for voting for 33 per cent of Leave voters). They played to a yearning for yesteryear common among older voters, 60 per cent of whom voted to leave. To the 'working class' voters who had been left behind by globalization and the free movement of people, they gave hope. They played to long-held feelings of British Exceptionalism. They also played to the most powerful emotion of all when it comes to politics: patriotism. A vote to Leave was a vote for Britain. Boris Johnson and co gave enough of the electorate the belief that Britain could not only stand on its own but, to borrow Donald Trump's meaningless yet highly successful slogan (a phrase he borrowed from Presidents Reagan and Clinton before him), that Britain could be 'Great' again.

Emotion trumps logic every time.

As the world now knows, it worked. The UK voted to leave the EU by 52 per cent to 48 per cent.

Emotion trumps logic every time.

It is interesting to note that voting in the referendum was split right down the middle in almost every possible way you could slice it – poor vs affluent, school leaver vs university educated, country vs city, England and Wales vs Scotland and Northern Ireland. Seventy per cent of Londoners voted to Remain. It has exposed a host of moral dilemmas. Should 52 per cent of those who voted have been enough of a hurdle for such a nation-changing decision? Should 16- and 17-year-olds have been permitted to vote (as in the Scottish independence referendum) seeing as it is their future we are affecting? Some 750,000 Commonwealth citizens residing in the UK were permitted to vote (and it is widely expected that most voted Leave) but 3 million EU citizens residing in the UK were not permitted to cast a ballot. A further 700,000 British expats who had been out of the country for 15 years or more were also not permitted to vote. This poorly planned plebiscite has divided – and changed – a nation forever.

Twenty-eight per cent of registered voters failed to vote in the UK referendum, 17.4 million voted to leave, 16.1 million voted to Remain and 12.9 million registered voters failed to vote. The UK has now left the EU because of the wishes of 38 per cent of registered voters who voted for several different types of Brexit – including a Norway-style model where the UK would remain part of the single market but not the customs union, a 'Norway-plus' model that includes a form of customs union, a Canada-style free trade agreement or a 'No Deal' Brexit that would see the UK leave and then begin to negotiate. As of late July 2020, every single one of these options is theoretically still on the table. The only mathematical certainty is that a majority of the UK population will be disappointed with whatever form of Brexit finally emerges.

Another reflection about Brexit is that Remain voters such as myself need to accept the change, move on and look for the opportunities. Let's keep that in mind when we get to the burning platform change curve in Chapter 10.

Of course, when it comes to change, what we need is a combination of both logic and emotion – with emotion used to enhance and build upon the logic.

To explore this a little further, let's take a look at the issue that so many of us grapple with on a daily basis – weight-loss.

Losing weight: when emotion and logic collide, emotion wins

Logically, losing weight should be a doddle. After all, the solution is simple. As a US friend of mine responded when asked how he had lost so much weight: 'I just stopped eating so freakin' much!'

Yet for the majority of us in the Western world, it is far from simple. In fact, our societies are in the midst of an obesity epidemic. Seventy-eight million adults and 13 million children in the US have to cope with the physical and emotional impact of obesity every day. Almost 40 per cent of US adults, 20 per cent of adolescents and children, and 1 in 10 preschoolers are obese, according to a report by the Centers for Disease Control and Prevention as reported by *NBC News* in October 2017. These are the highest figures ever recorded. Back in 1990, the figure for adults was only 15 per cent. This ratio has increased almost three times in the last 30 years.

Around 27 per cent of the population in the UK and Australia are officially obese. Most European countries sit in the low 20s.

The World Health Organization defines overweight as having a Body Mass Index (BMI) of between 25 and 30, and obese as having a BMI of 30 or above, which means that almost two-thirds of the English-speaking West is officially overweight or obese. Yes, BMI is imperfect (eg it takes no account of the fact that muscle is heavier than fat), but at least it is consistent. And let's be honest, pretty close to 10 times out of 10, if your BMI is over 30, then 'Houston we have a problem'.

The consequences of the obesity epidemic are devastating.

The consequences of the obesity epidemic are devastating. Obesity increases your chance of dying from COVID-19 by up to 90 per cent and is the second largest cause of cancer in the West. High blood pressure, diabetes, heart disease and stroke are not only killing millions of Westerners annually, obesity is also an incredible burden on health care systems – costing US $190 billion a year in the US alone, according to the report on *NBC News*. More people die from diabetes and sugar-fuelled cancers than those who are killed by war, crime, terrorism or suicide.[3]

These findings came on top of a World Health Organization report that childhood obesity is soaring around the world, having increased more than tenfold over the past four decades. Childhood obesity is linked to a higher chance of early death in adulthood.

The causes of this epidemic are (1) the kind of food we eat has changed significantly over the last few decades, (2) our relationship to food has also changed, and (3) we do less exercise.

The main reason is that we now eat far more processed, sugar-laden, 'low-fat' foods than ever before. Sugar is a killer. Quite literally. Our bodies turn half of it straight into fat – and it is everywhere in the modern, fast-food, preprepared diet. We also eat far more saturated fats than previous generations, drink fruit juice rather than eat fruit (which just pours fat-producing sugar down our gullet without the benefit of the fibre or the chewing) and consume far fewer vegetables.

Our relationship with food has changed over the last 50 years, mainly due to the ubiquitous availability of foods that are bad for us – and the compelling ways it is marketed and sold to us. We are bombarded by bad, cheap, processed and sugar-laden food constantly in the Anglicized West. Sugar is addictive and our species is hooked on it. Another phenomenon is that fat parents beget fat kids. I am not talking about 'fat genes', although genetics definitely play a role, I am talking about cultural/environmental influence. Kids who grow up in a household of fast-food, fried food and high-carb diets will inevitably be fat themselves. Probably for life. (Unless they are lucky enough to be helped by a wonderful charity called HENRY. More about this in Chapter 24.)

And we lead far more sedentary lives than previous generations. Our jobs are deskbound, we drive rather than walk or cycle, and our over-consumption of sugar makes us even more lethargic. Like any drug, as soon as the 'sugar rush' wears off, we crash back to Earth in need of another fix. The number of hours that we, and our kids, spend in front of screens these days only exacerbates the lethargy.

Actually, there's a fourth cause – sleep. An estimated 50 to 70 million Americans suffer from sleep disorders or sleep deprivation, according to the US Institute of Medicine. 'Sleep-deprived people may be too tired to exercise, take in more calories and may undergo hormones changes that control appetite', reports Dr Frank Hu, chair of the Department of Nutrition at the Harvard School of Public Health.

But are you ready for the really bad news? Diets don't work. And a growing number of us are waking up to this fact. Neuroscientist Sandra Aamodt was a serial dieter whose weight yo-yoed for 30 years. Her TED talk, based on her best-selling book, *Why Diets Make Us Fat*, boasts millions of views. I recently watched a brilliant short film of a similar nature entitled *Why Diets Fail*. It is part of the Netflix 'Explained' series. I highly recommend it.

The main reason why diets fail is because we think of them as short-term fixes rather than 'changing the way we eat forever' – and therefore we don't stick to them. An added obstacle is our body's innate protection mechanism; our natural metabolism is actually geared up to fight against rapid weight loss. *The Greatest Loser* was a US TV phenomenon that put extremely obese people through a televised boot camp to lose extreme amounts of weight. The average weight loss was 130 pounds (that's almost 60 kgs or 9 stone!). It was also a fabulous experiment on how a body reacts to such drastic weight loss. It rebels.

Six years after the TV show, the contestants had regained, on average, two-thirds of the weight they had lost. A big reason for this is that levels of leptin plummet if we lose weight rapidly. Leptin is a hormone that is produced by the body's fat cells. It effectively controls our metabolism, telling the brain that we have enough fat stored and that we can burn calories at a normal rate. When people diet, they lose fat cells, which decreases the amount of leptin in their system.

A low leptin level makes us hungry. 'Let's say you starve, let's say you have decreased energy intake, let's say you lose weight', explained Robert H. Lustig, MD, professor of pediatrics at the University of California, San Francisco and a member of the Endocrine Society's Obesity Task Force on the WebMD website:

> Now your leptin level goes below your personal leptin threshold. When it
> does that, your brain senses starvation and says: 'Hey, I don't have the energy
> onboard that I used to. I am now in a starvation state'. Then several processes
> begin within the body to drive leptin levels back up. One includes stimulation
> of the vagus nerve, which runs between the brain and the abdomen. The vagus
> nerve is your energy storage nerve. Now the vagus nerve is turned on, so you
> get hungrier. Every single thing the vagus nerve does is designed to make you
> take up extra energy and store it in your fat. Why? To generate more leptin so
> that your leptin can re-establish its personal leptin threshold. It causes you to
> eat and it causes you to get your leptin back to where it belongs.

The Greatest Loser contestants' leptin levels were tested after the competition and they had dropped almost to zero. Massive weight gain was inevitable. By the way, the bad news is that taking 'leptin supplements' doesn't boost leptin levels.

There's only one solution – lose weight slowly and sustainably.

To carb or not to carb?

If you want to lose weight, follow a low-carb diet, right? Maybe not! *Why Diets Fail* reported on a fascinating experiment where 609 volunteers who wanted to lose between 15 and 100 pounds were split into two groups. One group was told to follow a low-fat diet and the other group was asked to follow a low-carb regime. They were told not to count calories, just not to feel hungry. Everyone expected that the low-carb group would collectively lose the most weight. After all, that is what the Atkins diet and countless other programmes have been telling us for decades. Think again. The results for both groups were identical. The low-carb group lost as much weight as the low-fat group. The graphical distribution of weight loss/gain for each group was virtually identical.

It seems that the key to losing weight is located between our ears. By not fixating on counting calories, people actually ate less. Counting calories seems to focus the mind on what we are missing out on – and tricks our bodies into feeling hungry when it isn't.

The power of the mind.

The Netflix programme was concluded by Marion Nestle, Professor of Nutrition at New York University:

> Losing weight is quite simple... Eat fruit and vegetables. Not too much junk food. Avoid processed foods as much as you can and balance caloric intake with the kind of activity level you have. It really isn't more complicated than that.

So, the only way to lose weight is to eat less. Who knew?! But how?

The death of the calorie

The April/May 2019 issue of *The Economist*'s lifestyle magazine, '1843', featured an excellent article by Peter Wilson, a freelance writer based in

London. It explains how the meteoric rise of obesity in the West coincided with governments around the world adopting a US Senate committee report in 1977 that demonized fat and recommended a low-fat, low-cholesterol diet. The problem with low-fat foods is that they are tasteless – unless you add sugar, which all food manufacturers subsequently did with gay abandon. The article also reports how 'in 2016 a researcher from the University of California uncovered documents from 1967 showing that sugar companies secretly funded studies at Harvard University that were designed to blame fat for the growing obesity epidemic'.

Fat isn't bad. It leaves us feeling fuller for longer as our gut takes longer to break it down. Furthermore we need it to make hormones and protect our nerves. Sure, too much fat, especially saturated fat, will be a real problem: a bucket of KFC cannot be good for you! But what our bodies also don't need is excess sugar (and salt), which were the substances that the food industry started piling into the new low-fat foods we were being told to consume. Because excess sugar makes us fat.

And thanks to the food-industry-sponsored governmental advice, we all started counting calories. The problem with calories are: (1) not all calories are equal – sugars from processed foods and fizzy drinks are absorbed 15 times quicker into the bloodstream than the sugars produced from complex carbohydrates like cereals, pasta and rice; (2) labels on foods may understate their calories by up to 20 per cent; and (3) everyone absorbs and burns calories at a different rate due to a variety of factors (genetics, our personal gut microbiomes, the length of our intestines, how we prepare our food, the quality of our sleep, etc).

The only thing that works when it comes to weight loss is a complete change of lifestyle.

Countless studies have shown that counting calories can leave you feeling hungry and tired – and more than often doesn't work. Weightwatchers and Slimming World have both moved away from calories, focusing instead on sugar and saturated fat content.

The 1843 article goes on to suggest a simple alternative – throwing away the calorie counter books and eating a diet of natural foods: 'stuff from a real plant not an industrial plant'.

Diets don't work because they are short-term fixes. The only thing that works when it comes to weight loss is a complete change of lifestyle; a complete change of our relationship with food. And like all worthwhile change, that ain't easy.

And as we have seen, any successful and sustainable change requires us to address both logic and emotion – so let's look at both in the context of weight loss.

The logical part of the solution to losing weight

This part, to use Marion Nestle's words, is 'quite simple'. The top nine logical things to do to lose weight are:

1 Eat less.
2 Avoid sugar – which means avoiding processed foods, fruit juice, soft drinks, white bread, cakes, biscuits, cookies, almost anything low-fat, chocolate, ice-cream, ready-meals, sweets... as a friend of mine says, 'If it tastes good, spit it out!' (NB: I recommend a reality check with the use of the world 'avoid'. 'Minimize' or 'cut down' may be a better word. Eating needs to be enjoyable. If a new way of eating becomes a chore, it is unlikely to be sustainable and if it becomes an obsession, we take a step into dangerous territory. One of my many weaknesses when it comes to food is ice-cream. 'Avoiding' ice-cream completely would simply make life miserable, but devouring a half litre tub in one sitting – yes I could perhaps start to avoid that! Note to self.)
3 Eat as many vegetables as our hearts desire.
4 Eat fruit (especially as healthy snacks) but whole fruit not juice because the fibre is important. Fruit juice is liquid fructose.
5 Avoid fried food.
6 Reduce alcohol.
7 Drink lots of water.
8 Get proper sleep.
9 Exercise.

(Personally I find that cutting down on bread and dairy helps, too.)

This list is just common sense. Entirely logical. The vast majority of us know what we should do and yet we don't. I find it really tough to lose weight – and keep it off. It has little to do with logic or intelligence – some of the most intelligent people I know are obese, some dangerously so.

It has everything to do with emotions. Seeing as they are four times more powerful than logic, we must also address that pesky emotion-driven organ between our ears.

The emotional part of the solution to losing weight:

- We first have to want to change; genuinely want to change. (Remember the light bulb?) I cannot overstate the importance of this simple sentence. We only change if our desire is genuine. In this case our desire to lose weight needs to outweigh all of the other complex reasons why we eat and drink too much.

- We need to ask ourselves why we have consumed more than is good for us – and answer honestly. We need to honestly identify our current relationship with food. Then we may be able to think through how best to change it. Is our identity wrapped up in eating and drinking? Why? What can we do to reframe this identity (which, like all identities, is probably not real and only exists inside our heads)?

- We will need to create a sense of urgency – and convince ourselves that this is a change worth making – forever.

- We will need to understand that we are adopting a new attitude to food – permanently. The first step to changing an issue is to acknowledge its existence. Then we can start to reprogramme the way we look at consuming calories.

Creating new rituals is so important to making any sustainable change.

- We will need new habits, new rituals. Reaching for a cup of tea or a non-alcoholic drink rather than a beer at the end of a day. Ordering the salmon and vegetables more often than the 16oz ribeye with béarnaise sauce and fries. Stopping at one bottle of red rather than two. Or three. Getting out of bed and doing exercise three times a week before breakfast (note to self!). Creating new rituals is so important to making any sustainable change.

- We will need to find a substitute for eating more when we are tired; eating more when we are happy; eating more when we are sad.

- We will need to stop stocking cakes, sweets, soft drinks, chocolate, biscuits, cookies, fruit juice, processed meats, (even beer...?) in the house. We may have to force ourselves to reach for a banana or an apple or some nuts when snack time comes around.

- We need to reward ourselves when we achieve milestones – but not with food!
- We will need to stop judging ourselves and start liking ourselves a little more.
- We will need to give ourselves constant, but genuine, positive affirmation. I am a fab person. I will still be fabulous after the weight loss. Just lighter.
- We need to enjoy this new way of eating and drinking. It isn't a punishment. It isn't even a diet. It's a new way of living.
- We need to accept that results will take time and we will have to stay the course. This is a long-term, sustainable change we are talking about here. We shouldn't expect instant results (they don't last anyway – as we have seen). We will need to pace ourselves.

Do what I say, not what I do

In a blatant case of 'do what I say, not what I do', as I was researching this section, I calculated my BMI to be an ego-deflating 27.5 – smack bang in the middle of the official 'overweight' category – and duly (a) loathed myself and (b) sprang into action. I ate a tiny bowl of fruit and low-sugar yoghurt for breakfast washed down with two black coffees, went straight to the nearest pool and swam a kilometre as hard as I could (thinking I was still 25 rather than 55), ate a tiny plate of roasted vegetables for lunch, spent four hours hunched over my laptop forgetting to breathe properly or drink any water, then set off for a brisk walk (I was unable to run having torn a calf muscle a few weeks before, forgetting that it was decades since I last ran 10 km. Hmm there seems to be a pattern emerging here…) – and my body simply revolted. Pains across my chest (which turned out to be indigestion exacerbated by hunger, dehydration and bad writing posture) caused my overactive mind to think I was having a heart attack, which in turn made me break into a self-fulfilling clammy sweat and induced dizziness. My wife seriously thought of taking me straight to the hospital. In my quest for instant results, I had dehydrated myself, weakened myself, sent my blood sugar racing and placed myself into a situation that only two litres of sugar-infused water, lying down for three hours and a steak dinner was able to rectify. I ended up the day completely exhausted and heavier than when I started!

Don't be like me; go easy on yourself.

In the 'Be your own change leader' section at the end of part Five, I treat losing weight as if it were a change project as an example – and it produces some fascinating insights that will be useful for any personal change.

But first, let's round off the discussion on the power of emotion and then get stuck into looking at how we react to different types of change.

Emotional default settings

We all possess our own set of emotional and behavioural default settings – some good, some not so.

Our internal circuit boards are wired in a unique way. We may have a natural default setting to be ambitious – or content. Our natural inclinations may be to study hard at school – or not. We may be hard-wired to please. We may have an innate need to be liked.

Our environment also has a significant impact on our default settings. Children of divorced parents are more than twice as likely to get divorced than their peers, according to research quoted on mnn.com. Children growing up in welfare-dependent households are far more likely to end up on benefits than the national average. As JD Vance illustrates so starkly in his autobiographical novel, *Hillbilly Elegy*,[4] communities can develop default settings that infect entire neighbourhoods. In parts of the West that have been left behind economically, 'not trying' can become the norm – a default cultural setting can emerge that values failure over success and regards effort as counter-cultural, as 'not cool'. JD Vance lived through this in Kentucky. I have seen it in rural Queensland and parts of the UK; communities where Victimhood becomes the default setting. We will take a look at the common phenomenon of Victimhood and how to overcome it later in the book.

We can use our emotional default settings to our advantage. But the first step is to acknowledge their existence.

What are your emotional default settings?

PART THREE

How we react to different types of change

It's not what happens to you, but how you react to it that matters. EPICTETUS[1]

Change comes in many shapes and sizes. Sometimes it is planned. Often it is unexpected. Sometimes it is good. Sometimes it definitely isn't. All change is different. The only constant is that, somehow, we have to cope with it – no matter how big it is or where it came from.

For illustration purposes, I have shoe-horned the entire universe of potential changes into a neat 2 × 2 matrix. Doing this helps make sense of the subject. It gives us some context to help us analyse both our automatic reactions to different types of change and how we should try to react to change.

I have called it 'the Change Matrix'.

Let's take a look at it.

CHAPTER NINE

The Change Matrix

Simplicity is the ultimate sophistication. LEONARDO DA VINCI[1]

When I started to draw this simple four-box grid (Figure 9.1), my first thoughts were that the end result was going to be so 'Mickey Mouse', so painfully obvious and perhaps even patronizing that it would never see the light of day. I was wrong. The Change Matrix is now central to the Leading Change workshops I run for Henley Business School and I use it in every workshop on change that I run with leaders and employees in organizations around the world.

Its beauty lies in its simplicity.

All change can be characterized in terms of the size of the change (from big to small) and in terms of how much personal control we have over the change (from changes that have been done to us over which we have no control whatsoever, to changes that we have fully instigated and where we hold the controls). Obviously, there are any number of gradations along each axis, but let's just take a closer look at the extremes.

Adapt: Lurking in the bottom left-hand corner of our matrix, we find small changes that are forced upon us. I have called this box 'Adapt'. The changes in this box could be as trivial as a change of date when you have to put the bins out to a minor change to the recruitment process at work.

FIGURE 9.1 The Change Matrix

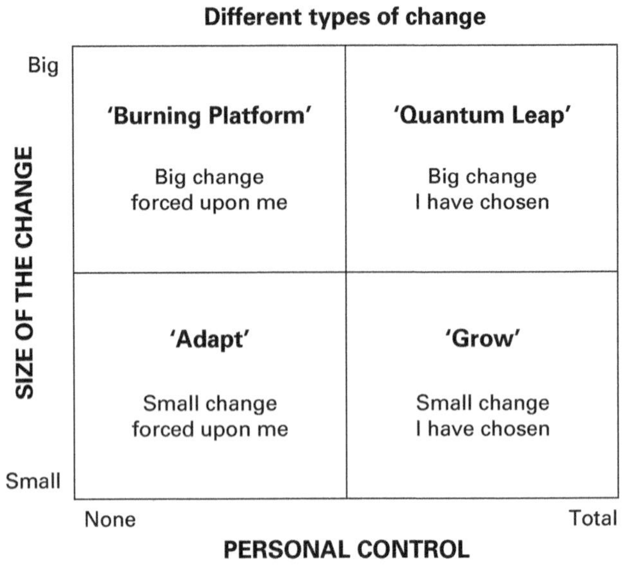

Different types of change

We may not be in control of the changes, but the alterations and effort required of us are not significant. We simply get on with it.

Grow: Sticking with small changes, let's move sideways to the bottom right-hand quadrant where we find a cluster of small changes that we have consciously brought about ourselves. I have called this box 'Grow'. The changes that live in this quadrant could be a change of wardrobe or hairstyle or changing a process at work that was entirely in our remit to make. They are small and they are changes that we have instigated.

So far, so good.

Now let's move further up the 'size' axis. That's where things become more complicated, more daunting and far more interesting; for the consequences of these changes increase exponentially in line with the size of the change.

The larger the change, the larger the impact of the consequences of the change.

Burning Platform: This is the earthquake square; the top left-hand corner where lives unrequested and often unexpected change – change that rocks our world and shakes our confidence; change that can feel like a sickening blow to the solar plexus; that can cut us off at the knees. It is big change that has been done to us.

I call this the 'Burning Platform' quadrant from a phrase attributed to change consultant and author, Daryl Connor, in 1998, as he watched a news report about workers jumping from a burning oil rig in the North Sea. The fact that their physical oil rig was literally aflame was the sole reason they jumped. They had no choice. They had, quite literally, a 'Burning Platform for Change'. While this is a powerful metaphor, I don't subscribe to the theory that in order to bring about change we have to make the status quo so uncomfortable that even leaping into an ice-cold, tempestuous sea seems favourable in comparison. Being 'encouraged' to jump off a burning oil rig does not mean that we will eagerly embrace the freezing cold waters below. We may comply with the need to change, but we will be highly reluctant swimmers! But it is the ideal metaphor for this sort of big, scary, emotional, unrequested change.

Big change that is thrust upon us can arrive in many forms – cancer, the death of a loved one, losing your job, becoming divorced, being in an accident, or even winning the lottery. (Several studies have shown that winning the lottery doesn't make you any happier; in fact it can even take away the pleasure of everyday activities such as having breakfast or hanging out with friends. Mind you, we only have the researcher's word for this. I think I would prefer to experience a lottery win for myself before being able to confirm or deny the alleged lack of increase in happiness... but I digress.)

Quantum Leap: Finally we head east to the top-right quadrant – large changes that we have instigated ourselves. I have called this the 'Quantum Leap' quadrant. It is a leap into a new world, most often with a host of significant consequences. Some of these consequences we may have been able to predict, but many of them will be unforeseen – known unknowns (ie consequences we know we don't know) and even unknown unknowns (consequences we haven't even dreamt of yet). And we will have to learn to cope with all of them.

The changes found in this quadrant could be a promotion, a new job, a new career, moving to a different part of the country or even a different country altogether. It could be deciding to marry or perhaps even deciding to divorce. It could be deciding to come out. It could be deciding to change your gender. This sort of change is exciting – and you have instigated it.

But it will still be more than a little bit scary. All change, even change that we have brought about ourselves, is challenging. Because all significant change requires giving up something; requires stepping out of our comfort zone. A promotion requires giving up your current relationships with your colleagues. A house move requires leaving your neighbours and friends. No significant change is easy – even when it is 'good' change. But if we don't change, we stagnate. Furthermore, it is far better to be in some control of the change rather than have change entirely thrust upon us.

If we don't change, we stagnate.

While countless forests have been felled to describe and analyse 'Burning Platform' change, very little attention has been paid to 'Quantum Leap' change. But as we will see, the changes in the Quantum Leap quadrant can also be incredibly challenging – even though we have instigated the change – for we undergo an emotional roller-coaster that is rather similar to the emotionally draining ride we experience in the world of the Burning Platform.

Let's discover what happens when we are confronted with both of these types of big change that is forced upon us – the world-shattering 'Burning Platform' change and the what-on-earth-have-I-done 'Quantum Leap' change.

Let's explore how we naturally react to both.

CHAPTER TEN

The 'Burning Platform' Change Curve

There are no mistakes, no coincidences. All events are blessings given to us to learn from. ELISABETH KÜBLER-ROSS[1]

How we react to 'Burning Platform' change... big change that is thrust upon us

A great deal of research has been done on how people instinctively react to 'Burning Platform' change (Figure 10.1). One of the clearest, simplest and most useful methods of describing these reactions is 'the Change Curve', first introduced by Elisabeth Kübler-Ross in her 1969 book *On Death and Dying*. It has also been called 'the Grief Curve'.

Figure 10.2 is my version of Kübler-Ross's curve, modified for business. Our reaction to unexpected change is highly personal and yet also rather predictable. When we are faced with change that is thrust upon us, our natural reaction is to proceed through eight different sequential stages. Each and every one of us goes through the same process. The only difference from person to person is the amount of time we spend in each stage before moving on to the next one. It's automatic. It's normal. We all do it.

Shock is our initial reaction when confronted with an unexpected change. If it is a small change, this step may be over in the blink of an eye.

FIGURE 10.1 The Change Matrix: the Burning Platform

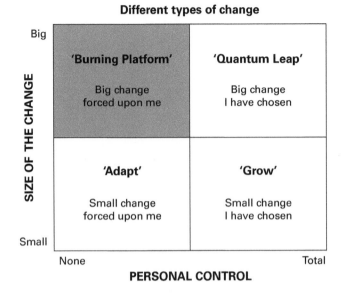

Different types of change

	Big	
	'Burning Platform' Big change forced upon me	**'Quantum Leap'** Big change I have chosen
SIZE OF THE CHANGE	**'Adapt'** Small change forced upon me	**'Grow'** Small change I have chosen
	Small	
	None	Total

PERSONAL CONTROL

FIGURE 10.2 The Burning Platform Change Curve: for change that is done to us

THE 'BURNING PLATFORM' CHANGE CURVE

Our reaction to **change that is done to us** is both personal and predictable.

Modified Kübler-Ross change curve

Shock
Denial
Anger
Fear
Depression

Acceptance
Understanding
Moving On

Resistance | Frustration | Trough | Exploration | Adoption

Large changes, however, can really set us back in our tracks and we can remain in a state of shock for some time. In extreme situations, shock can cause the body to freeze or even shut down. When we are in a state of shock, we become deaf and dumb – we aren't really paying attention; we aren't processing a great deal. And once the shock wears off, we can be left feeling utterly exhausted.

Denial inevitably follows. We tell ourselves that the company's leaders will come to their senses and change their minds about the proposed restructure. We tell ourselves that someone our age can't get cancer; that the diagnosis must be wrong and we need a second opinion. This simply cannot be happening! Denial is a highly powerful emotion. Once it takes root, it can be difficult to budge.

But perhaps, to some extent, it is necessary. The inventor of the Change Curve, Elisabeth Kübler-Ross, saw a value in Denial: 'Denial helps us to pace our feelings of grief. There is a grace in denial. It is nature's way of letting in only as much as we can handle.'

Eventually its hold on our psyche dissipates and we will be able to move on to the next stage – when we really get to vent our frustration.

Anger is invariably next. Once we finally start to admit that the change is real, we get angry and we search for someone or something to focus our anger on; someone or something to blame. In our need to rage at the injustice of it all, we can say or do things that sometimes we may later regret. We rage against God or gods various. We rage against the government. We rage against our employers. We rage against ourselves. When it comes to organizational change, more leaders need to understand that this anger is an automatic, natural and predictable reaction to big change that has been thrust upon us. Leaders need to treat people with understanding and empathy while they are passing through the inevitable 'anger' stage of the Change Curve.

Anger often masks deeper sets of emotions – hurt, pain and more often than not, fear.

Fear either arrives hot on the heels of anger or it is the underlying cause of it. We fear the consequences of the change – and remember that we are talking about a big change that has been done *to* us. We fear the pain of chemotherapy; we fear for our family's future if we die; we fear death itself. We fear that we may not get another job; we fear for our family's financial future; we fear for our self-esteem and self-worth. Fear of the future is a perfectly normal and completely understandable reaction to significant, unrequested change. Knowing this may not make it any less painful, but at least we can derive some small comfort in the fact that it is completely normal. It's OK to be afraid.

The healthy thing to do during this phase is to vent your frustration; air your fears; get them out on the table. Often, they loom larger when trapped between our ears than they do after they have been voiced and subject to harsh daylight. It is also cathartic. When it comes to organizational change, I implore leaders to actively seek out the fears and concerns of their people, as it is the only way that they have a chance of moving forward and embracing the change. And besides, the leaders will undoubtedly learn something in the process.

During the 'Anger' and 'Fear' stages we may also find ourselves bargaining, trying to avoid the change by doing deals with either the instigator of the change or ourselves. 'If I take a pay cut or work three days a week, we could cancel the redundancy'; 'If I stop eating meat, maybe the cancer will go away.'

Depression is how we feel in the trough of the curve and it is another normal reaction. Perhaps we should really label this phase 'Depressive State' because the negativity we feel when we are in the trough can range from feeling low to anxiety to fully blown Big-D Depression. As Kübler-Ross discovered, before we can even think of moving on, we need to grieve. Grieving isn't weakness. It can be painful, sometimes excruciatingly so, but it is a necessary part of the healing process. When you reach this stage of the curve, this trough, you will feel awful. It can feel like a deep, dark and foreboding space in which to be, however necessary. But be careful that your negativity while in The Trough doesn't lead you off in one of two self-destructive directions: self-blame or victimhood.

You may blame yourself for everything that has been done to you. If you end up in this mode, your weaknesses, as you perceive them, will be crystal clear and loom large. Self-loathing may even ensue. In my Leading Change workshops, I implore business leaders to empathize with their people as they traverse the Burning Platform Change Curve, to understand what their people are going through, and to give them a break. Give them a break when they are angry; give them a break when they are fearful; give them a break when they are in The Trough. You will need to do the same thing – give yourself a break and realize that your negative feelings, however raw and all-encompassing they may feel are firstly, normal, and, secondly, just feelings. They will pass. Honest. Be grateful for what you have. Look for the positives. Continue to believe in yourself.

Be grateful for what you have. Look for the positives. Continue to believe in yourself.

The trough on the Change Curve is where victims dwell. When change is done to us, it is very easy to succumb to the insidious, cold-comfort lure of victimhood.

Victimhood is so insidious and so powerful that it is worth dedicating a few pages to exploring the phenomenon in a little more detail – as well as what to do when you find yourself slipping into victim mode.

The cold comfort of victimhood

If it's never our fault, we can't take responsibility for it. If we can't take responsibility for it, we'll always be its victim. RICHARD BACH[2]

Sometimes, when big change is done to us, we wrap ourselves in the comfort blanket of victimhood. It is actually a false, cold comfort; but comfort, nonetheless. If we are not careful, victimhood can even become part of our identity.

We all know people for whom victimhood is their default setting. They seem to attract rotten luck. In fact, they expect it. Deep down, they may even come to think they deserve it. They feel hard done by with their career, their health, their bodies, their opportunities, their relationships, their lives. And it's someone else's fault.

This is the insidious and seductive nature of victimhood. It places the blame onto someone or something else. But this is a dangerous con trick and a slippery slope. For the more we identify as a victim, the less competent we actually become.

Victimhood can strike any of us. It can feel like a comfortable place to be if we aren't ready (or don't want) to take responsibility. But it's insidious.

The only way out of this black hole is to recognize that you are thinking of yourself as a victim and then try to reassert some control – or at least influence – over events.

When we are in victim mode, we fool ourselves into thinking that some-one else is solely responsible for our current predicament. But worse, we fool ourselves into thinking that someone else is responsible for our future, too; that someone or something is preventing us from action. This is very dangerous – for the last thing we are, even when the chips are down, is powerless.

We possess the power to take control; the power to change.

Reframe your way out of the trough

Today you can make the decision to no longer be a victim; of your past, of your mistakes, of your failures, of your bad relationships, of your financial situation, of your weight, of your health, of other people's opinion of you and even of your own negative self-worth. This day in this moment, you can decide to no longer be a victim and start being a victor. EDDIE HARRIS JR[3]

Victimhood can creep up on you when you least expect it – especially when change is being done *to* you. The only escape route starts with realizing what has happened, that you have descended into victim mode. Don't judge yourself for it, just observe it.

Then you can start to change your mindset and approach.

Escaping the 'victim triangle'[4]

Often when people enter victim mode, they do two things: they search for someone to blame (a 'Persecutor') and look for someone to comfort them (a 'Rescuer').

A Persecutor can be real or imagined – sometimes even a little of both. It is the boss that has made you redundant. It is the bully at school. It is the over-bearing and incompetent manager. It is the abusive husband.

Genuine Persecutors have almost always been persecuted themselves, have little self-esteem and feel that attack is the best line of defence. Underneath the bluster, they actually see themselves as victims. They are small-minded people in positions of power. Often, power that we have given them through our reactions.

A Rescuer is someone who loves rescuing people. We all know them. With all the best intentions, they are the first to comfort people when they are being victimized. On the surface they appear to be angels – ready with a box of tissues, a warm cuppa and bucket loads of empathy. But scratch the surface and you will often find that Rescuers aren't really helping. In fact, they love rescuing so much that sub-consciously they end up keeping the victim in their place – so that they can keep on rescuing.

When I explain this phenomenon in my Leading Change and Embracing Change workshops, I always ask the delegates, 'So, how do we escape this Victim Triangle?' The best answer I have heard is: 'Become a Persecutor!' This quick-witted quip was actually chock full of insight. This is precisely what a large number of victims do; knowing no other course of action, they go on the attack and find someone else to victimize or to turn the tables on the Persecutor. This simple comment helps to explain why victimhood and persecution tend to follow one another. But of course, this isn't breaking out of anything – it is perpetuating the negative, empty and unproductive state of victimhood.

Breaking out of this vicious triangle requires the victim to (1) realize they are thinking of themselves as a victim, (2) acknowledge that this is highly self-destructive, and (3) take control by reframing the entire situation – looking at the situation in a completely different manner.

A strategy called 'The Empowerment Dynamic'[5] describes just such a way that we could do this. It recommends that the victim adopts the alternative role of 'Creator', views the Persecutor as a 'Challenger', and enlists a 'Coach' instead of a Rescuer. I like this approach because it puts the soon-to-be-ex victim in the driver's seat. It implicitly gives them control.

Rather than looking at yourself as a victim, start to consider yourself as a 'Creator'. Creators focus on outcomes not problems.

Start to regard your persecutor as a 'Challenger' – rather than persecuting you, they are *challenging* you, in effect daring you to reassess the situation and to do something about it. They may not be doing it in a very collegiate or constructive manner, but try to ignore how they are behaving and look at what they are suggesting as though they were trying to help. After all, there are only two things you can actually control: your thoughts and your actions. Regard these taunts as challenges and act accordingly.

There are only two things you can actually control: your thoughts and your actions.

Look around you and see if a friend or colleague is displaying 'Rescuer' behaviours. Is someone trying so hard to rescue you that you aren't able to rescue yourself? Are they smothering you with kindness but in a way that perpetuates your feeling of being a victim? If so, you need to get this 'false positive', negative energy out of your life. The last thing you need is a 'Rescuer'.

What you may need is a Coach – someone who asks questions that are intended to help you to make informed choices. The key difference between a Rescuer and a Coach is that the Coach sees the Creator as capable of making choices and of solving their own problems – and helps them to do just that.

So... be a Creator of your own opportunities, see Persecutors as Challengers and look for a Coach. It is damn good advice whether you find yourself in a victim triangle or not.

And by the way, sometimes the best coach is you.

After the trough

Understanding is the first step on the road to a brighter future. It's the logical part of the upward curve. Understanding of the situation in which we find ourselves; of the reasons why it has happened; of the process ahead; of the options available to us; of the skills and tools we have at our disposal; understanding of our next steps.

Acceptance is a step further. Understanding happens in the head. Acceptance happens in the heart. It's the emotional part. Once we have logically laid out where we are, the options available and the actions we need to take, we can move onto full acceptance of it. We need to jettison the last lingering remnants of denial, anger, fear and depression and accept that this has indeed happened. We need to engage our emotions – constructively. Then we can start to assert some sort of control and embrace the future.

Moving on doesn't mean forgetting. It may not even mean forgiving. It means precisely what is says on the tin – moving on. It's action time. We have realized we are not powerless in the face of this change. What we now choose to do as a result of this change is completely within our control. And any residual pain will recede over time.

It is worth noting that the Change Curve is not one-way traffic. When it comes to big change, we may slide up and down this curve several times. Neither is it a once-in-a-lifetime experience.

A pause for reflection

Let's pause to take a breath for a moment.

Take a little time to think of a major change that was done to you and now re-read the words associated with each step of the 'Burning Platform' Change Curve, reflecting on your own experience. How long did you spend in a state of shock? How deep was your level of denial? How did your anger express itself? What were you afraid of? When did you hit rock bottom and how did you feel when you did? How did you start the journey out of the trough and your head begin to understand? Did you slide back into the trough? If so, how many times? When did you realize that your heart had started to accept the change? How liberated did you feel once you actually moved on?

You will never forget the change or how it made you feel at the time. You may never forgive the perpetrator either. But has the intensity of the feelings waned over time? Every cloud has a single lining – what was yours? What did the change end up enabling you to do that you would otherwise not have done? What would you have done differently if you had your time over again?

Next time a change happens to you, reach for the Change Curve and recognize that your reactions are normal. Be as objective as possible. Observe how you react to the change, and do this objectively, without criticism. Watch yourself travel through each stage and guide yourself through the journey.

Next time change happens to those around you, do precisely the same thing. Use the Change Curve to help them make sense of what is happening to them. With this simple tool, you have the power to help them to make the most of the situation and transport themselves through the curve to a brighter future.

CHAPTER ELEVEN

Personal reflections of reacting to Burning Platform change

Change isn't a project with an end date.
The Change Curve isn't something you can navigate
once and put behind you.
It is a part of life. CAMPBELL MACPHERSON

We have all been forced to cope with big change that is forced upon us. I'd like to take this opportunity to share a few personal reflections of my own – and some observations of how my inspirational wife and incredible children have coped with Burning Platform change.

If you look at my bio at the start of this book or the detailed version on www.changeandstrategy.com, you could be forgiven for thinking that my working life has been plain sailing and forever upwards – one triumph after another. After all, my CV reveals that I am an award-winning author, international business adviser and keynote speaker, and that I have had senior executive roles with fascinating companies in exotic locations across the globe… but, as always, it is what is *not* in the CV that is often far more interesting. Life is never plain sailing. The Change Curve is omnipresent.

In my long and varied working life, I have had several completely different careers (my last career change was in 2017 just before my 54th birthday and it won't be my last) in a dozen different industries, several dozen different jobs and 19 employers since leaving school. I have been sacked once and been made redundant three times.

The time I was sacked did not come as a surprise; a salesperson who had ceased to make sales should not expect to be employed for too much longer! So when I was shown the door, I skipped the Shock phase completely. I also raced past Denial and Anger as well as I had no-one to blame but myself. But Fear kicked in big time. I was 28 and although I had a degree and had flown a military jet solo (long story), I had pretty much nothing to show for the previous 10 years. I still refer to it as my 'lost decade'. I left school on a fantastic high; full of promise and opportunity and I had utterly failed to live up to anything even close to my potential. I was a 'failure'. You can tell I was well and truly stuck in the trough of the Curve at this juncture.

While in the trough, a friend called to tell me that he had also been sacked and had an idea to start a business selling interactive brochures on floppy disks. It was late 1991. Colour laptops had only recently been invented. No-one had heard of a CD-ROM and the internet was still a military secret. So I borrowed some money and 'InterMark' (interactive marketing) was born and I set about selling a new concept based on new technology in the middle of a recession. It wasn't long before I was back in the trough of the Change Curve. While we had some initial success with the likes of Nissan, American Express, Singapore Convention Centre, Axa, Pfizer, AMP, Zurich and even Apple coming on board as clients, I learnt the hard way just how difficult it is to grow an under-capitalized business – especially one that didn't own its intellectual property and didn't charge enough. The stress of just paying the wages bill every month became so unbearable that by the time that we 'sold' the business to a large advertising agency, my then business partner collapsed from a nervous breakdown. (And when I say 'sold', I really mean 'put on the payroll'!)

There were times during the InterMark days when I would drive home at lunchtime, close the door and scream with utter frustration and despair. Several times I ended up in tears, before gathering myself together and getting back to the office. When you are in The Trough of Depression, sometimes all you can see is the steepness of the slope ahead of you – with no discernible way of climbing out.

It seemed that every time I did manage to clamber out, something would turn up to push me back down again.

In conjunction with one of Australia's greatest golfers, Jack Newton, we designed and built an interactive golf tutorial in 1993. It was brilliant. We signed up Nick Price, who had won the 1992 US PGA, and launched 'Nick Price's Troubleshooting Golf' in the United States. We sold 50,000 copies and my personal share of the royalties from this was to be US $300,000. I had finally made it. Three months went by and no commission had been forthcoming from our agent in Los Angeles. During the fourth month, on 17 January 2004 to be precise, Los Angeles was hit by a devastating earthquake. Our agent's office building was completely destroyed. He disappeared to South Africa, never to be heard of again. With our money.

This wasn't the last time I have had to navigate my way through the Change Curve. And it won't be my last, either. So, what keeps me going? An innate burning desire to achieve something certainly helps. I know people who have suffered similar blows and have retreated into the trough and wrapped themselves in the cold comfort of victimhood never to return. I have certainly donned the cloak of victimhood from time to time. I have certainly 'wallowed' (as my wife calls it) when something has gone wrong and I have also suffered from 'neg attacks' (yes, another one of Jane's) – but rarely for long, even though they can be unbearably intense at times. The reason is that I simply don't see victimhood or wallowing as a viable alternative to taking stock and doing something; to getting back on the horse, maybe a different horse, and charging off once more. Life's simply too short and, besides, failure is life's way of teaching you stuff. Failure, setbacks, bad times, are all just part of life.

Failure is life's way of teaching you stuff. Failure, setbacks, bad times, are all just part of life.

No-one gets away scot free.

Like father like son

My wonderful son, Charlie, learnt this aged 18. Having aced his Year 11 exams, he was forecast top marks for his final end-of-school results. He was all set to go to Edinburgh University to study chemistry. Until results day.

He was stunned. His teachers were stunned. The results he achieved were not enough to study chemistry at any of the universities to which he had applied. He had, in his mind, 'failed'.

And the Burning Platform Change Curve hit him with the force of a Mack truck.

He immediately went into Shock. The school that had been such an important part of his life for the previous seven years was no help whatsoever. A teacher handed him his results envelope, sucked air through his teeth and said, 'With those results, you can forget any Russell Group university.[1] Clearing closes at 3pm so you have six hours. You better get online and hit the phones'. None of the teachers shuffling aimlessly in the back of the hall would look my son in the eye. They were only prepared for success. They had no idea what to do in any other situation. But worse than that, they just didn't care.

Charlie briefly slipped into Denial during the car journey home, followed by Anger at his teachers and the school for their complete lack of empathy and assistance on this crucial day and then Fear – not so much fear of what he was going to do but fear of how he was going to face his friends that evening at the end of school party. Fun, popular, clever Charlie was a 'failure'. He was well and truly into Depression by the time we got home.

He forced himself out of the trough long enough to 'hit the phones' and rang a dozen Russell Group Universities to ask if there was any way he could be accepted. The answer was no. Back into the trough he plummeted and he could see no way out.

This is the moment when we need help. And this is the moment that his mother and sister leapt into action. Jane found something called a 'foundation year' that a handful of universities offered for precisely this situation. She also decided to search for universities outside of this 'Russell Group' that offered chemistry. She discovered that Sussex University, not a member of the Russell Group, was actually rated no.1 in the UK for the subject. Emily then learnt that Sussex had a foundation year in biochemistry and Charlie was coaxed out of his trough to call them. Within minutes, they had offered him a place and guaranteed him a room in one of the halls of residence. The crisis was over.

And yet pushing through the Change Curve is never quite that simple. That evening at the party he slumped back into the trough. The fact he hadn't got into any of the universities of his choice still hurt.

He slipped back into an even deeper trough during his first week at university as well. Knowing no-one, living in dire digs and about to start a foundation course that he still thought was for 'losers', he had never felt so lonely or so worthless. The phone call he had with us was heartbreaking. But there was nothing we could do. Or to put it more accurately – doing nothing was the only good thing we could do. He had to take ownership of the situation. Only he could find his way out of his trough. To his utmost and enduring credit, he finally admitted this (Understanding) and then genuinely believed it (Acceptance). He rang two days later and told us that after wallowing for a few hours immediately after our phone call, he had stood up, looked at himself in the mirror and given himself a damn good talking to. He took a deep breath, pushed his shoulders back and ventured out into the social maelstrom that is Fresher's Week, having decided to give it 'the full Charlie', introducing himself to as many people as he could with a genuine smile and welcoming disposition.

He has never looked back. He learnt to study, aced the foundation year, was accepted into the chemistry degree course, became Social Secretary of Men's Hockey and joined the drama club. In his first year, he won the Sussex University Dramatic Society's award for Best Supporting Actor. In his second year, the mothers of two of his closest friends died and he was there to help them cope with the most enormous of Burning Platform changes. He was elected President of the Hockey Club, twice, and was nominated for Sports President of the Year, and even secured a small part in *1917*, a Stephen Spielberg/Sam Mendes feature film. He has now left university with a 2:1 BSc in Chemistry and gongs for Club of the Year, Committee of the Year and the University of Sussex Leadership Award. He is off and running.

And a great deal of his success stems from learning to cope with big, unexpected change.

Like mother like daughter

My incredible daughter, Emily, learnt to cope with Burning Platform change at an even earlier age. She was diagnosed with juvenile idiopathic arthritis (JIA) when she was just seven. Her young body's immune system was so hyperactive that it was attacking her joints – and the pain was horrible. Rather than catching a cold whenever she was run down, one of her thumbs would swell up and become immovable, a knee would puff up to two or three times its normal size and her neck would seize and ache from within. She was in almost constant pain. And she had to take drugs to help dampen her immune system; low-dose cancer drugs like methotrexate (side effects of methotrexate include nausea and liver problems), strong anti-inflammatories and steroids – drugs that no child should have to take. From her mid-teens onwards, she was injecting herself every week with Etanercept.

This was enormous change that had been thrust upon her. And she spent her childhood sliding up and down that damn Change Curve. There were times when she collapsed in floods of tears, wanting to be rid of the pain and dreading the next time she had to have fluid removed from her knee (a painful procedure) or a steroid injection directly into the knee (an even more painful procedure).

And yet she never let it beat her.

JIA is a condition that many children grow out of – but not all – and Emily experienced so many false dawns where she thought it had fled her body only for it to come back with a vengeance. Her doctors announced that she was officially 'inflammation free' aged 21 in 2017 having slowly reduced her drug dosage over the preceding few years. She then contracted glandular fever and it was like a defibrillator had been applied to her immune system – off it went into over-drive again.

She has learnt to cope with all of this and not to be defined by her condition. JIA isn't her. It's just something she has. She has learnt to accept it and to live her life around it. She has learnt to listen to her body and hear when it is asking her to lay off the alcohol or to get some sleep. At university she got fit and took up yoga to keep herself strong – and to help her put it all into perspective. She also decided to seek out help – from a nutritionist, a gut specialist, an acupuncturist, an osteopath and a GP who thinks holistically. She is 24 and she is stunningly beautiful, confident, intelligent, sunny, fit – and well.

She has an economics degree from York University, where she was editor of the *Economics* magazine, did an internship with PwC and a sustainable quant fund in London and has moved to Sydney where the warm weather agrees with her body and nourishes her soul. She has just joined JPMorgan as an ESG and Equity Research Analyst and has her whole fabulous life ahead of her.

Jane and I are not just bursting with pride about what she has achieved in her young life to date. We are even more proud of how she has achieved it. She is an inspiration.

Like daughter like mother

But our experiences pale a little in comparison to what my wife went through aged 13. One minute she was living an idyllic life in the south of England with her two brothers, her glamorous ex-BOAC hostess mother and her clever father who was working for the World Bank. Then the phone rang. Her father had suffered a heart attack and drowned off a beach in Indonesia. Their idyllic world fell apart.

The next half a dozen years were unbelievably tough in the Purvis household as they struggled to fill the gaping hole in their lives; struggling through the Change Curve over and over again. Much tougher than anything I have ever experienced. My mother-in-law, who somehow brought up three children single-handedly to see them all become fabulous adults, found solace and strength in Christianity, from her dear friends at Wives Fellowship and from the fellow worshippers at her local church. My wife, Jane, found solace and strength from within. She became determined. This was about the most difficult change anyone could be asked to cope with and cope she did. Yes, she was incredibly upset and at times swamped by sorrow, but she refused to think of herself as a victim and was determined to do what her father always wanted her to do – which was to go to university.

She worked hard through school, obtained a business degree from Manchester University (the exact same course at the exact same university that her father had attended she would discover years later), went to work for Ogilvy & Mather and then took herself off to Sydney for what was supposed to be a two-year break aged 25. She would stay 10 years and go on to be the Head of Promotions for Pepsi, Head of Sponsorship & Donations for Westpac Bank (winning the right to be the banking sponsor for the 2000 Olympics), Head of Brand Strategy for Barclays, give birth to two amazing children – and marry me (not necessarily in that order).

Jane can cope with any change. She learnt how to do that 40 years ago and has proven it time and time again in the 29 wonderful years that we have been together. She is now a truly sublime yoga teacher and fully quali-fied yoga therapist with many years of experience in both. She helps people cope with change through yoga every single day. Some of the changes she has enabled people to enact are truly remarkable. She helps people perform miracles.

I may be a little biased, but I think she is one herself.

The 'Burning Platform' Change Curve is not something to navigate once and forget about it. It is something we all have to do continually throughout our lives again and again.

It is a part of life.

CHAPTER TWELVE

The 'Quantum Leap' Change Curve

Even 'good' change involves a loss of something; letting go
of something we value.
Even 'good' change can feel like a leap into the unknown.
CAMPBELL MACPHERSON

How we react to 'Quantum Leap' change... change that we have chosen

Surprisingly, the way we react to major change that we have instigated ourselves is rarely straightforward. Even though it is change we have wanted and have made happen, we go through a similar emotional roller-coaster. Let us look again at the Change Matrix, but this time at the 'Quantum Leap' quadrant (Figure 12.1).

Pause to think about when you have instigated big change – deciding to get married, having a baby, buying a house, moving house, changing jobs or going for – and getting – that promotion.

While Kübler-Ross's Change Curve is an invaluable aid to reach for when change happens *to* us, it doesn't quite cut the mustard when it comes to change that we instigate. So, I have adapted her brilliant tool again, this

FIGURE 12.1 The Change Matrix: the Quantum Leap

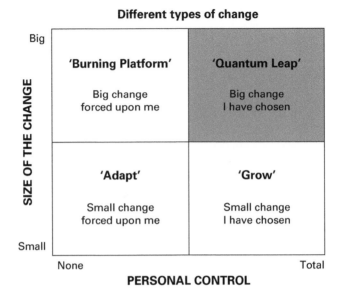

Different types of change

FIGURE 12.2 The Quantum Leap change curve: for change we instigate

time to construct a change curve that documents our automatic and normal reactions to major change that we have chosen ourselves. Welcome to the Quantum Leap Change Curve (see Figure 12.2). It is shallower than its sibling and almost as powerful.

Excitement is the first emotion we experience when it comes to significant change that we have instigated. A promotion! A new school! A new house! A new job! A new business! Marriage! Anything new is always exciting. Our psyche revels in the excitement of it all – for if it didn't, we would never make the decision to change. For a while, the excitement is all we can see. But even when it is good change that we have set in motion, doubts and fears can often be found lurking in the shadow of the excitement.

Even when it is good change that we have set in motion, doubts and fears can often be found lurking in the shadow of the excitement.

Apprehension is the next feeling to surface. I know it will be exciting but what about all the details? Where and when are we going to hold this wedding? Have I got enough money? What if there's something wrong with the house? Will I succeed at this new job? Will I be able to pull off the promotion?

One of the concerns about getting a promotion at work is what David Rock, Australian neuroscientist, calls 'a loss of relatedness'. Remembering that even good change means a loss of something – the successful candidate suddenly not only has a new status but this new status inevitably means that the relationship with their old peers will change. This is difficult. Some new team leaders never recover and wish they had never been promoted in the first place. Moving house, moving school, going to university are all examples of emotional changes that result in a loss of relatedness.

And frequently, apprehension amplifies itself and turns into...

Fear. Fear of the future is not exclusively reserved for change that has been thrust upon us. It is also a normal reaction to 'good' change; change we have chosen. It seems counter-intuitive that good change will cause us to fear or to panic, but it does. One of my closest friends in the world was one of the youngest ever full directors of Rothschild's Bank. In fact, he had to wait until his 30th birthday before Sir Evelyn would allow him to become a director. A year or so after, I asked what he thought about when he looked in the mirror every morning. 'Do you really want to know?' he replied. 'I think "Today is the day they are going to find me out".' This feeling is called Imposter Syndrome and is a ridiculously common reaction to promotions – in all walks of life. Why organizations don't expend more effort in helping newly promoted people to be successful perplexes me.

A few years ago, I was fortunate enough to be granted a three-year contract with one of the world's largest Sovereign Wealth Funds, based in Abu Dhabi. It was a full-time engagement with a highly respected organization that would do wonderful things for my career and my bank balance. It would see me flying all over the globe in style and enable me to live in a fascinating and exotic part of the world. Best of all – I could avoid the drab English winter for three consecutive years! I was over the moon with excitement. But, and there is always a 'but', it would mean massive change for my family. Our tightly knit nuclear foursome would, after 16 fabulous years, be subjected to abrupt and premature change. My move would mean that our son would choose to start boarding school. Our daughter was heading off to university, but I was leaving first and the move would mean that Jane and I wouldn't be in the country to help her if necessary. Even though we all decided that it was the right thing to do, I sat on the plane heading for the Gulf full of apprehension and a crippling fear that I had made the wrong decision. I then inevitably slipped into remorse (and then progressed through the rest of this change curve as the flight continued).

Remorse is a strange and inescapable phenomenon when it comes to change – even good change. 'Buyer's Remorse' is a well-known reaction that occurs almost every time we buy something. Maybe the Samsung was a better television. I am not sure I even like the house anymore – and we haven't even moved in! Is he really the one I want to spend the rest of my life with? Seller's Remorse is the other side of the coin but just as common. Did I get the best price? Why did I say yes? What was I thinking!?

Rational optimism. Rather than the 'understanding' stage of the previous curve, I have called this stage 'rational optimism'. We learn that the decision we have made is not all beer and skittles. Every upside has its downside. Every silver lining has a cloud. Every decision comes with its own set of consequences. We learn that this new business may take a while to get off the ground. We learn that this new phone may take some getting used to. We learn that we have to study and go out of our way to make friends at university. We learn that we have work to do to make the change successful.

But we are optimistic anyway. Our head has kicked in and rationalized that even with all of the consequences we now know are there, we can do this. We can triumph.

Genuine belief. And then we accept it. If we are to get on with the change, rational optimism must morph into the deeper, heartfelt feeling of acceptance; accepting the consequences of what we have done and reacquainting ourselves with the reasons why we took the plunge in the first place. Acceptance is a fabulous state. By reaching this stage, we have

Every upside has its downside. Every silver lining has a cloud. Every decision comes with its own set of consequences.

transformed heady excitement into reality. Acceptance allows us to make informed plans and executing these plans allows us to...

Embrace the change. We can now get on with embracing and executing the change. We can start to make it real. In my case, it meant disembarking the plane and literally stepping into a whole new world.

CHAPTER THIRTEEN

Life in the Quantum Leap Change Curve

We must have perseverance and above all confidence in ourselves.
We must believe that we are gifted for something and
that this thing must be attained. MARIE CURIE[1]

Allow me to introduce you to one of the most impressive and inspiring people I have had the privilege to meet.

Dr Bronwyn King, AO, is a force of nature. Her energy is infectious. Her story is inspirational. The intensity of commitment to her mission can, at times, be overwhelming. But then her mission is overwhelming, too.

She is out to convince and assist the world's major financial institutions to stop investing in tobacco; an addictive substance that kills more people in a month than illegal drugs, guns and war combined in a year.

To describe her mission as ambitious would be the under-statement of the decade, for she is up against two of the most formidable opponents imaginable – cancer and the all-powerful tobacco industry. This is her story. So far.

It is the story of how many of the world's largest financial institutions are beginning to avoid an industry whose products kill many of its customers painfully and prematurely.

But it is also an inspirational story of the trials, tribulations and joys of bringing about genuine, meaningful change; of someone who has been sliding up and down the Quantum Leap Change Curve since 2010.

Let me first set the scene, because Bronwyn's story is both fascinating and inspiring. 'The tobacco epidemic is one of the biggest public health threats the world has ever faced, killing more than 8 million people a year around the world.'[2]

Let me try to put this horrendous number into some perspective:

- The 9/11 terrorist attack on New York killed almost 3,000 people. Tobacco killed 3,000 people before 3:15 on the morning that you're reading this book. The death toll from tobacco is the equivalent of seven 9/11 attacks every single day of the year.
- Around 50,000 Americans die of opioid overdoses every year. It is a shocking tragedy. For every one opioid death, there are 10 deaths from tobacco.
- An estimated 200,000 people die prematurely from drug use globally every year, according to the United Nations Office on Drugs and Crime – mainly opioids but also cocaine, heroin, methamphetamine and the like. This is considered to be so devastating to our societies that it warrants our governments spending billions every year waging 'wars on drugs'. Tobacco kills 200,000 people every nine days. Where is the 'war on tobacco'?
- 250,000 people are the victims of non-war-related gun deaths globally every year. Tobacco kills that many people every 11 days.
- The holocaust was one of humanity's darkest hours. Six million innocent people were slaughtered. Tobacco kills as many people as the holocaust every nine months.

On average, smokers die 10 years earlier than non-smokers, according to the US Center for Disease Control and Prevention (CDC). CDC also declares that tobacco kills almost half of its users. This means that smokers are effectively playing Russian Roulette but with bullets in every second chamber; for while one in two smokers will live long lives (albeit often plagued with numerous health problems) the other half will die, on average, 20 years early – 20 years.

CDC estimates that more than 500 million smokers alive today will die prematurely as a result of their smoking – 500 million preventable, premature, often painful deaths.

And through our pensions and investments, many of us have been profiting, albeit unwittingly, from all this carnage. For ever since the formation of joint stock corporations, the global financial services industry has been an enthusiastic supporter of the manufacturers of this deadly product; a product that has killed three people in the time it has taken you to read this sentence.

Until now.

The moment an oncologist discovers she is investing in tobacco

Dr Bronwyn King received the Order of Australia for 'distinguished service to community health' in January 2019. As an elite swimmer, she represented Australia and was Team Doctor for the incredibly successful Australian Swimming Team from 2002 to 2010. But it is her chosen field of oncology in which she is changing the world – and in ways she never expected.

Dr King began working in the radiation oncology department of Melbourne's world-renowned Peter MacCallum Cancer Centre in 2001. Her life-changing moment came one day in 2010, after yet another day of battling against tobacco-induced cancer, during a routine meeting with a representative of the hospital's superannuation (pension) fund. Dr King was shocked to discover that a significant proportion of her savings, and those of all of her colleagues at the hospital, was being invested in tobacco companies. As Bronwyn recalled:

> We are the biggest cancer centre in the southern hemisphere. One-third
> of cancers are caused by tobacco and here we were, all of these doctors
> and nurses, spending our lives fighting cancer, only to find that our money
> was being invested in the very companies whose products were killing our
> patients!... I was speechless. After the representative had left, I just stood in the
> café for a few moments in a state of shock, processing what he had told me.

Dr King's next step was to present the news to her colleagues:

> Every Friday afternoon at the hospital one member of the radiation oncology
> team was tasked with presenting an interesting case to the rest of the team.

My 'interesting case' presentation was coming up about three weeks after I discovered we were investing in tobacco. So, instead of presenting a clinical case, I presented this.

She alerted everyone to the fact that they were all supporting the tobacco industry with their long-term savings. She then looked directly into the eyes of each one of her colleagues one at a time and said, 'You own Phillip Morris. You own British American Tobacco'. To the Professor of the lung cancer unit, she declared, 'You own Imperial Tobacco'. 'This is what has been happening with our money and it's been happening as long as we've been working here. I don't think it's a great fit', she ended, with world-class under-statement.

The Head of Radiation Oncology was equally dismayed and said, 'You need to tell the CEO'. So she did. He then arranged for her to present to the leadership of Health Super, the specialist pension fund that invested the savings of thousands of health workers across the State of Victoria:

> This was another league entirely. I was a doctor. I knew nothing about finance. I had no idea how to speak 'finance'. I did a lot of homework to learn about the industry but I was still an amateur. About an hour before the meeting, I rang my dad and I said, 'Could you just pronounce the word fi... fi... could you just pronounce it for me?' I googled how to pronounce the word 'fiduciary'. I'm ringing my dad, and he's pronouncing it, and then I said, 'Now, can you just put it in a sentence for me?'
>
> So we had the meeting. The hospital's CEO, our Head of Media Communications, the CEO of Health Super, their Chief Investment Officer – and me.

And nothing happened.

The hospital reached out to the other super funds they had relationships with. The meetings were positive but, again, little action was immediately forthcoming. 'I was incredibly frustrated. Doing nothing was a genuine risk for our hospital brand. Doctors, nurses and allied health staff were all inadvertently investing their money in tobacco and yet we were a leading voice on anti-tobacco and anti-cancer.'

And 2010 went by without any discernible movement, much to Bronwyn's dismay. Then, in mid-2011, she was invited to present to the entire boards of Australia's two largest superannuation funds for health workers, accompanied by the Professor from the lung cancer unit and Peter MacCallum, CEO.

She talked about how the fund members cared for the community, how the funds themselves sponsored anti-cancer campaigns and simply said:

> You are representing us. You do these great things and yet they are totally conflicted by how you invest. You invest on behalf of the health industry. You represent the doctors and nurses who deal with cancer every day. It doesn't work.

What I love about Bronwyn's approach is that she doesn't play the blame game. She is passionate about the subject but she doesn't let her emotions tip over into anger or vitriol. She innately knows that such an approach would simply force people to be defensive and cause them to find all sorts of reasons why they can't or won't change. Her lack of emotional attack gave them room to move, time to consider. It gave them a way out, a path to change:

> I knew that meeting went well because of a beautiful moment that occurred immediately afterwards. We walked out after the meeting and a Board Member chased me out of the room, catching up with me before I had reached the lift. She chased me out to say, 'Just so you know, my mum died of lung cancer. Thank you so much for doing this'.

That is how most of Dr King's meetings have ended ever since:

> If there are more than three or four people in the room, someone will chase me out to the lift. If they don't quite make it, they email me that night and say, 'Just so you know, I was in your presentation today. I didn't say anything. I was the third guy down on the left. My Dad died of lung cancer when I was 15 years old. I have never recovered. All power to you. Go for it'.

However, even with a visceral reaction from some of the board members, the decision to remove tobacco companies from Health Super's portfolios took another year (it was merging with a much bigger fund, First State Super, to form a US $35 billion asset manager) and divesting of tobacco stocks was certainly not an easy decision to make.

A pension fund's first responsibility is to manage retirement savings on behalf of its members – and delivering a financial return is, of course, the core reason for the fund's existence. Tobacco is, after all, a legal product. Did the fund's board have any right to make these sorts of moral judgements? Could such an action actually be in contravention of their fiduciary duty? Superannuation funds, by law, are required 'to act in members' best interests', which until quite recently has been interpreted in a purely financial sense. After all, they are in the money management business.

'I understand that initially a few Directors were undecided. However in the end, after considerable investment modelling and much discussion, the Board was united in its resolve to eliminate tobacco from all portfolios', Bronwyn said.

Timing was also on her side. Australia's pioneering 'Tobacco Plain Packaging Act' was announced in 2011 to go live on 1 December 2012. 'I could tell the board that these were stocks whose product was being condemned and restricted by every government around the country', recalls the CEO of First State Super, Michael Dwyer. 'I told the board that tobacco stocks had no redeeming feature.'

While it would take another five years before tobacco shares would peak and start to plummet worldwide, many Australian funds saw the writing on the wall in 2012 and concluded that tobacco looked like a questionable investment for genuine long-term investors.

On 19 July 2012, First State Super announced that it was removing tobacco from all of its portfolios. Not just the portfolios of health workers but from every single one of its funds.

'I was on maternity leave', recalls Bronwyn. 'I got a phone call the day before, from the CEO of the hospital, saying, "Just so you know, it's going to be in the paper. They're doing this." I put the phone down and was in a bit of shock. "Oh, my goodness, they're doing it!"'

It was two and a half years since that fateful meeting with her pension fund. But she had done it. Health workers all across Australia would no longer be investing in tobacco. My question to her was: Why didn't she just stop there?

> Because I knew that if one of them could do it and it was the right thing to do, then they all could. First State was the third biggest fund in Australia. They'd done it and the press was extremely positive. They felt great. So others could, too. But I had no idea what to do next.
>
> So I wrote a 'Thank You' letter to Michael Dwyer and asked if I could meet him. Michael has since become my mentor. He is a very, very special person. We got on like a house on fire. He could see that it was an issue that was worth pursuing, and he also knew that if he could do it and his fund could do it, that there was no reason why the others couldn't as well. And he overwhelmingly felt it was the right thing to do. Our first meeting finished with him saying,

'Look, if I told you I was going to Darwin next month for a conference of all of the government related pension funds in Australia, and if I said we could do a speech on this together, what would you say?' I said, 'Book me a ticket'.

That's when things really got going.

From Australia to the world

By 2016, Bronwyn had persuaded 35 Australian superannuation funds, controlling nearly half of the total funds under management, to remove tobacco from their portfolios. By the end of 2018, Australian funds that control a total of US $1.3 trillion of assets had gone completely tobacco-free.

However impressive this figure is, Australia is a small part of the global economy. Australian funds make up just 4 per cent of the total global pension funds under management.[3] To fulfil its mission, Tobacco Free Portfolios needed to spread its word internationally.

And it did – starting with the world's second largest insurance company, AXA. Like many insurers, AXA had struggled with the inherent conflict of being a health insurer that also invested in tobacco. 'Tobacco had been a problem for Health, but it had not been a problem for investors', explained Sylvain Vanston, AXA's Head of Corporate Social Responsibility. 'When I met Bronwyn, she immediately started putting together the pieces of the puzzle that we hadn't. She asked us: "Would you set up or invest in an industry now knowing that in the next year it would kill millions of people and cost global health care systems a trillion dollars?"'[4]

AXA's incoming CEO, Thomas Buberl, needed little convincing. 'Decisions take longer when they're ambiguous', says Buberl. 'There is nothing ambiguous about tobacco.'[5] He had been arguing that the insurance industry needed to change from being an industry that paid medical bills to an industry that helped clients make healthier life choices. And of course, there was also a financial aspect to the decision: advances in medicine have transformed lung cancer from a quick death sentence to a lethal, lengthy, chronic – and expensive – illness.

The day before Easter 2016, Bronwyn received an email from AXA. It simply read: 'We have decided to go tobacco-free. If you can, let's discuss further. Thanks for your help'.

Two months later, standing next to Dr King at a gathering on the eve of the World Health Assembly in Geneva, Thomas Buberl announced that they were selling 200 million euros worth of tobacco stocks and running down 1.6 billion euros of tobacco corporate bonds.

Tobacco Free Portfolios had gone global.

The Pledge

The Tobacco-Free Finance Pledge is an initiative for financial institutions to formalize their commitment to 'be part of the solution to ensure a tobacco-free world for present and future generations'.

By signing The Pledge, organizations commit to work together to raise awareness of the issue of lending to, investing in and insuring tobacco companies; and to encourage the adoption of tobacco-free finance policies across lending, investment and insurance. The Pledge was formally launched on 26 September 2018 at a 'High-Level Side Event' on the sidelines of the UN General Assembly at United Nation's Headquarters, New York, in partnership with the Principles for Responsible Investment, the UN Environment's Principles for Sustainable Insurance, the UN Environment Programme Finance Initiative and four Founding Financial Partners – BNP Paribas, AXA, Natixis and AMP Capital.

Tobacco Free Portfolios was now a UN-supported global initiative.

Doing good vs doing well

> *Clients expect me to exercise an investment judgment*
> *not a moral judgment.* NEIL WOODFORD[6]

The financial services industry outside of Australia, New Zealand, Canada, The Netherlands and the Nordic countries finds the decision to stop investing in tobacco a challenging one – especially in the UK and the United States. Tobacco may kill millions of people a year and the industry may exploit the young (80–100,000 children start smoking somewhere in the world every single day, according to the World Health Organization and 'in impoverished tobacco growing communities, child labour is rampant',[7] according to the International Labour Organization), but it is a legal product and tobacco stocks are firm members of the main UK and US indices.

If you invest in funds that track the FTSE 100 or the Dow Jones, you invest in tobacco. Having worked in the international financial services industry for several decades, I know that a moral argument alone is insufficient. It must be accompanied by an airtight financial justification. Asset managers need to be shown that their portfolios can deliver the same if not better returns without tobacco – so that they are able to 'do good *and* do well' by avoiding tobacco stocks. (And they can. Dutch civil service scheme ABP made a 20 per cent profit on the divestment of stakes in tobacco producers and the nuclear arms industry in 2018 – a gain of 700 million euros for its pension account holders.)

If you invest in funds that track the FTSE 100 or the Dow Jones, you invest in tobacco.

'You cannot be a "responsible" or "sustainable" investor in tobacco', explains Dr King. 'You are either "in", which means that you want the companies to grow and succeed and thrive and find new customers, or you are "out".'

Nest, the workplace pension scheme set up by the UK government is pulling out of tobacco – for performance reasons. Nest manages more than £10 billion on behalf of more than 8 million savers who are auto-enrolled into default company pension schemes. Mark Fawcett, Nest's chief information officer, believes that the business model of the tobacco industry looks increasingly unsustainable:[8]

> We've been highlighting our specific concerns around tobacco investments and its performance for a couple of years now. Tobacco companies are facing legal challenges across the world from governments taking action against an industry causing serious harm to their citizens. The harsher regulatory environment stops tobacco companies from attracting new customers and increasing their market share of existing smokers. In our opinion, tobacco is a struggling industry which is being regulated out of existence.[9]

With smoking on a dramatic and perhaps chronic decline,[10] doubts whether vaping will fill the long-term revenue gap (no matter how many new addicts these new e-cigarettes create) and increasing legislation and community concerns over both smoking and vaping, questions abound over the attractiveness of tobacco stocks as a long-term investment.

If asset managers don't need to invest in tobacco to generate superior returns for their clients, they can stop providing finance to companies whose products kill millions of people and cost our societies billions.

Everybody wins.

Dr Bronwyn King and the Quantum Leap Change Curve

'I have travelled up and down that Change Curve more times than I care to remember', admitted Bronwyn:

> My very first reaction to the discovery that I was investing in tobacco back in 2010 was 'disillusionment', which spurred me into action. The Quantum Leap Change Curve kicked in when Tobacco Free Portfolios was formally established in 2015. I distinctly remember the feeling of 'excitement' of creating this new entity to fix something important that needed to be fixed.
>
> The apprehension you describe arrived when I realized that I had never done anything like this before. I had no idea how to speak 'finance' or how to approach pension fund CEOs. 'Daunting' didn't cover it. Have I doubted myself? Countless times! And I have definitely been in that trough a few times – wondering whether I have bitten off more than I can chew. But I move myself on as quickly as possible. My years as a competitive swimmer taught me that success is up to me. No-one can do it for me. While an occasional rest in the 'trough of remorse', as you call it, may be inevitable; it is unhealthy to linger there for any length of time. So I don't.
>
> I am incredibly lucky that I have the support of my family, my Tobacco Free Portfolios team and many mentors who keep my spirits high and energy focused. The incessant travel takes a toll on everyone, not to mention the financial burden, which has been very significant.

Changing the world is not for the faint hearted.

The Empire strikes back?

Change is rarely easy and never linear. Every change initiative is a roller-coaster, with troughs following peaks with an almost predictable frequency.

When it comes to leading change, I advise my clients to ask themselves 'What could possibly go wrong?' and plan accordingly. So I asked Dr King whether Tobacco Free Portfolios is ready for the inevitable challenges that lie ahead; whether she is ready for the inevitable backlash once the purveyors of 'cancer sticks' start to react to her success, and whether the pension funds and asset managers will hold their nerve.

For the last couple of years, the stock market has made it a great deal easier for asset managers to divest of their holdings in tobacco – tobacco shares have plummeted. By mid-June 2019, shares in the big three tobacco firms (Altria, Philip Morris (PMI) and British American Tobacco (BAT)) had lost a third of their value.

Meanwhile, tobacco companies have been working hard to change the perception of their industry; adopting the language of responsible capitalists, speaking of 'Next Generation and Potentially Reduced-Risk Products' such as 'oral tobacco and nicotine markets'. They are also keen to point out that:

> The tobacco industry remains a substantial contributor to the economies of many countries and the livelihoods of millions of people across the globe, including farmers, retailers and those employed in the tobacco supply chain.[11]

Tobacco companies are incredibly profitable and they use their vast cash mountains to pay high dividends (as of late 2018, BAT was paying a whopping 7 per cent dividend yield[12]) and acquire non-tobacco companies (including newly emerging legal marijuana companies and e-cigarette firms). They proclaim they are morphing from tobacco companies into 'lifestyle' conglomerates that just happen to have tobacco divisions.

Philip Morris International has even hired a globally respected sustainability guru, Professor Robert Eccles of Oxford University, to advise them on matters of 'sustainability, social impact and investor engagement'. Professor Eccles is a great choice. He was the founding Chairman of the Sustainability Accounting Standards Board and Arabesque Asset Management, an ESG fund. In 2011, he was named as one of the world's 'Top 100 Thought Leaders in Trustworthy Business Behavior', and in 2014 and 2015 was declared to be one of the '100 Most Influential People in Business Ethics'.

Dr Eccles' job appears to be to encourage investors to engage with the industry rather than exclude it – an approach that explicitly conflicts with the principles and values of both the UN and the World Health Organization.

In a detailed article on LinkedIn, entitled 'Solving the cigarette problem',[13] Professor Eccles claims that he was unaware that (a) nicotine was the addictive component of cigarettes, and (b) that it was 'the burning of tobacco that actually kills people'. This surprisingly naïve and awfully convenient positioning enables him to praise PMI's efforts to promote '(potentially) less harmful mechanisms for delivering nicotine to smokers, such as heated tobacco products and vaping'.

Will tactics like these be enough to placate the consciences of institutional investors? Will an alleged corporate 'transformation', coupled with high dividends and a vision of future growth from e-cigarettes and marijuana be sufficient for the investment tide to start to flow back again?

What will Dr King have to do to help global pension funds, asset managers and asset owners to 'keep the faith'?

The tobacco industry is deploying its vast armies of PR, marketing and legal professionals to distract investors and lawmakers from the fact that their products are lethal.

We cannot be complacent. We cannot stop reminding ourselves of why we are doing this. We cannot stop reminding the pension funds, institutional investors and fund managers who have signed The Pledge as to why they are doing this. We cannot stop spreading the word among the rest of the investment community. We simply cannot stop.

With collective annual revenues of some US $760 billion (and that figure excludes the enormous Chinese market!), the tobacco industry is deploying its vast armies of PR, marketing and legal professionals to distract investors and lawmakers from the fact that their products are so lethal. They are continually looking for new ways to give institutional investors excuses for investing in them; to help them to hold their noses and take the dividends. They are even trying to position themselves as being part of the solution! The PMI PR machine is working in overdrive, declaring a dream of a 'smoke-free future' and providing funds to the 'Smoke-Free Foundation' whose stated purpose is 'to improve global health by ending smoking in this generation'[14] – all designed to give themselves an air of social responsibility. To me, this is little more than a smokescreen, pardon the pun.

Dr Vera da Costa e Silva, Head of the WHO FCTC Secretariat, is far less charitable:

> For many years, global tobacco's ruling barons have cloaked themselves as good global citizens, softly spoken executives well-versed in the reassuring language of corporate social responsibility. They have masqueraded as partners for decent and well-meaning programmes designed to improve the lot of the world's poorest and most vulnerable. And you can see what they gain: an

invitation to speak to decision-makers at the highest levels, which offers an aura of respectability and feeds the narrative of responsible partnership. This is a lie.[15]

PMI's attempts to position itself as a responsible corporate citizen, ironically with the wellbeing of its customers at the heart of its business, is disingenuous for two reasons.

First, tobacco is killing almost a million people every six weeks. Hundreds of millions of people will die from tobacco before any tobacco company genuinely becomes 'smoke-free'. And second, 'smoke-free' is a fatuous phrase. 'To many it might sound beneficial, perhaps even good for you, but what does it actually mean? Does it mean tobacco-free? No. And it certainly doesn't mean safe!' explains Dr King.

The industry is making a big deal about their 'heated tobacco' products or 'vaping' as it is commonly known. Vaping is the tobacco industry's magic bullet; the potential answer, they hope, to their own corporate longevity.

But what is it? And how dangerous is it?

Vaping is an aerosol created by heating a liquid concoction of chemicals and nicotine that users inhale. 'The vapor is made of fine and ultrafine particles which have been found to contain propylene glycol, glycerin, nicotine, flavors, tiny amounts of toxicants, carcinogens, heavy metals and metal nanoparticles among other substances.'[16]

In the words of Dr Michael Blaha, MD, MPH, Director of Clinical Research at the Johns Hopkins Ciccarone Center for the Prevention of Heart Disease, 'You're exposing yourself to all kinds of chemicals that we don't yet understand and that are probably not safe'.[17]

On 22 August 2019, the US Centers for Disease Control and Prevention reported 193 potential cases of severe lung illness tied to vaping in 22 US states, including one adult in Illinois who died after being hospitalized. Three weeks later, the number of deaths had grown to eight and President Trump declared that vaping should be banned. Putting aside the interesting fact that eight deaths prompted this sort of response when 40,000 Americans die from gunshot wounds every year and 500,000 annual deaths from tobacco elicits no response whatsoever, if The White House were to ban vaping, tobacco company share prices would be in the doldrums forever.

It didn't. As of February 2020, the number of recorded deaths in the United States attributed to vaping had reached 68 and the number of vaping-related illnesses and injuries was greater than 2,800, including one double lung transplant. Caused by vaping.

Vaping is a highly efficient way for tobacco companies to distribute a highly addictive and dangerous drug. As Dr Blaha explains:

> Nicotine is a toxic substance. It raises your blood pressure and spikes your adrenaline, which increases your heart rate and the likelihood of having a heart attack. Many e-cigarette users get even more nicotine than they would from a tobacco product. You can buy extra-strength cartridges, which have a higher concentration of nicotine, or you can increase the e-cigarette's voltage to get a greater hit of the substance.

It is also a lucrative way to get a new generation hooked on nicotine. Twenty per cent of US high school students have already taken up vaping, according to CDC.

'What I find most concerning about the rise of vaping is that people who would've never smoked otherwise, especially youth, are taking up the habit', says Dr Blaha. 'It's one thing if you convert from cigarette smoking to vaping. It's quite another thing to start up nicotine use with vaping. And, it often leads to using traditional tobacco products down the road.'

With its talk of a 'smoke free future', its moves into 'heated tobacco products' and the diversification of its businesses into cannabis and other industries, the tobacco industry is working hard to distract attention from the fact it manufactures addictive and harmful products that kill 8 million people every year. It is doing its best to muddy the waters and give investors reasons to pause before divesting.

The tobacco industry employs more than a million people worldwide, generates more than US $2 billion a day of revenues and leverages its massive cash mountain to pay massive dividends and try its best to control the worldwide media agenda.

Dr King is without a doubt on the side of the angels, but her battle is far from over.

Lessons on change from Dr Bronwyn King

There are so many invaluable take-aways from Dr King's inspirational and ongoing story. Here are some of the main ones.

Be crystal clear about the 'why' and the 'what'

When you bring about big change yourself, when you jump into a new venture that will change your life in dramatic and profound ways, the first thing is to be crystal clear about why you are doing this and what you are trying to achieve. And be honest with yourself.

To Bronwyn, the 'why' was startlingly clear. Once she discovered that she, as a dedicated oncologist, was inadvertently investing in the very products that were killing her patients, she simply had to act.

What is she trying to achieve? 'To significantly reduce and one day to even stop the world of finance propping up the manufacture of tobacco.'

And it is important. When the Director General of the World Health Organization heard of Bronwyn's mission, he declared that 'tobacco-free finance' was 'the missing piece of global tobacco control'.

To change successfully, we need to harness the power of emotion.

Believe in yourself

It's easy to back yourself when you are doing something you have done many times before. The trick is to believe in yourself when you are venturing into unknown territory. Understand that you will travel through the Quantum Leap Change Curve – and back again. Your excitement will be tainted by doubt and apprehension, perhaps even a little fear. You may even find yourself in the 'trough of remorse' for a period or two. But with a healthy dose of self-belief, your head will present you with all of the logical reasons why you can do this, your heart will discover all of the emotional reasons as to why you can and must do this – and you will embrace the change head on.

Never give up

'Not every investor and fund manager I meet is instantly convinced by my explanations and arguments', admits Dr King:

> Some have tried to postpone decisions or detailed discussions on the matter, saying: 'Oh it's a bit early' or 'Can you come back with more information?' But I've watched literally dozens of people move from a position of initial resistance, confident that theirs is a reasonable position, to being completely

convinced and ringing up a few months later asking: 'Is there anything I can do to help you spread the word… I never hear 'no' as 'never'; I hear it as 'not yet'.

Be emotional but respectful

To change successfully, we need to harness the power of emotion, and it doesn't matter if it is ourselves we are trying to change or others; this must be done respectfully. It needs to be done in a way that is free from blame and vitriol.

As agents of change, our job is to help people to want to change – for people only genuinely change if they genuinely want to. That is equally true for you, as you are your best agent of change.

How you communicate is as important as what you communicate

Knowing that intense enthusiasm and fervour can sometimes distract from the message and even cause people to harden their resistance, Dr King has been very careful with the words she uses. She isn't an 'activist'; she is an 'oncologist'. She tries to veer away from 'fighting a cause' or being on a 'crusade' (words I inadvertently used in the opening section of this chapter). Financial institutions are 'partners' rather than 'targets'.

She leaves her ego behind and continually puts herself on the same side as the people she is trying to influence – because there is simply nothing to be gained by confrontation.

> I presented to one fund that took sustainability very seriously. They chose their 'sustainable investment' option using the Dow Jones sustainability index – an index which, despite its name, ironically included British American Tobacco. When I pointed this out, the board members felt tricked. Before I got home, I had an email from their CEO saying, 'We've issued a comprehensive tobacco-free mandate across our portfolio'.

It was *how* Bronwyn helped them to uncover this killer fact, without blame or point-scoring, that made their change possible.

Ask yourself: 'what could possibly go wrong?'

No plan ever goes according to plan. As German military strategist Helmuth von Moltke (1800–91) proclaimed, 'No battle plan survives contact with the enemy'. Mike Tyson explained it a little more colourfully: 'Everyone has a plan until they get punched in the mouth'.

Every strategy, every change, comes with its own set of implications and consequences. Yours will too. The first part of the solution is to do your utmost to explore ahead of time what the potential implications are likely to be. The second part is to be completely clear about what you are trying to achieve and your reasons for instigating the change, so that when unseen consequences arise – as they will – you are ready, willing and able to deal with them.

CHAPTER FOURTEEN

Returning to The Matrix

The best place to hide is in plain sight. EDGAR ALLAN POE[1]

Let's return to our Change Matrix to summarize all we have discussed in this part (Figure 14.1).

Adapt: For small changes that have been forced upon us, we need to strive to accept the change and put it into perspective. By definition, it is a small change. Sure, we didn't ask for it, but let's not blow it out of all proportion.

Grow: For small changes we have chosen – crack on with it and keep it coming. It is called continual personal development; an essential component of success in our personal life as well as our many careers.

Burning Platform: For large changes that have been forced upon us, we must use all our resources to push through the Kübler-Ross Change Curve, avoiding victimhood, until we get to acceptance – so that we are ready, willing and able to embrace the opportunities that will inevitably present themselves.

Quantum Leap: For large changes we have brought about ourselves, we need to prepare, experience The Change Curve, embrace the consequences and execute.

FIGURE 14.1 The Change Matrix

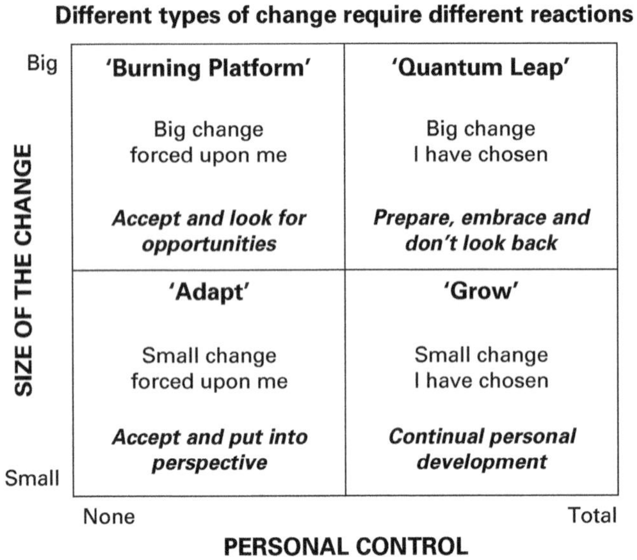

Different types of change require different reactions

	None → Total (PERSONAL CONTROL)	
Big	**'Burning Platform'** Big change forced upon me *Accept and look for opportunities*	**'Quantum Leap'** Big change I have chosen *Prepare, embrace and don't look back*
Small	**'Adapt'** Small change forced upon me *Accept and put into perspective*	**'Grow'** Small change I have chosen *Continual personal development*

SIZE OF THE CHANGE (vertical axis: Big to Small)

None — Total

PERSONAL CONTROL

A blinding glimpse of the obvious

It wasn't until I actually used The Change Matrix with a client that it revealed its hidden secret to me – a secret that was hidden in plain view. As the keynote speaker for the Bibby Group's CEO conference on change, I was in full flow extolling the virtues of the Matrix, when one of the CEOs called out, 'Stop!… I have just worked out why most of our change projects fail', he said, looking at The Change Matrix that was projected 10 feet high on the wall of the conference room. 'It's because we leaders are in the Quantum Leap quadrant but our people are over in the Burning Platform square!'

This was a brilliant piece of insight. For the change leaders who are instigating the change, their change curve starts with Excitement. For the change followers who are having change done *to* them, their change curve starts with Shock.

FIGURE 14.2 Leaders and followers inhabit different parts of the matrix

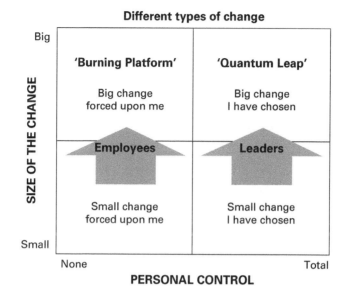

The Change Matrix brings into stark relief why there is almost always a chasm of understanding between the leaders of organizational change and the rest of the organization that is being tasked with the implementation of the change. Too often, change leaders simply don't understand why the rest of the organization isn't as enthused or as excited as they are. Perhaps a glance at The Change Matrix will help (Figure 14.2). This simple realization may make it easier for change leaders to understand and empathize with the people they are asking to 'get on board with the change'.

Too often, change leaders simply don't understand why the rest of the organization isn't as enthused or as excited as they are.

The aim of any change leader should be to get these two arrows as close together as possible, and this requires empathy, communications and genuine engagement. People can only start with Excitement if they have been involved in the planning of the change.

PART FOUR

Overcoming the barriers we erect to change

The world hates change, yet it is the only thing that has brought progress. CHARLES KETTERING[1]

Resistance to change is normal. Our instinctive, knee-jerk reaction is to resist it. Our in-built change resistance is one of the main reasons why 88 per cent of corporate change initiatives fail.

(The other reasons why the majority of business changes falter fundamentally boil down to leadership – lack of clarity of what they are trying to achieve and why, poor understanding of the implications of the change, an obsession with process over outcomes, complacency, inertia, the 'set up to fail' syndrome, poor communications and disingenuous stakeholder engagement, forgetting that emotions trump logic every time, a change-averse culture and a leadership that doesn't stay the course. Details of all this and more can be found in my book *The Change Catalyst: secrets to successful and sustainable business change*, Wiley, 2017.)

In all aspects of life, not only while we are at work, we automatically erect our own personal barriers to change. We all do it. Every one of these barriers is emotional and every one is completely normal. We try to convince ourselves they are insurmountable barricades, but they're not. They are merely obstacles that we put in our own way. Barriers we can overcome. And in this part, we will explore how to do just that. We will explore how to:

- Admit **Denial**
- Harness our **Emotions**
- Confront our **Fears**
- Find good **Tribes**
- Reframe our **Identity**
- Test our **Doubts**
- Detach from our **Negative Thoughts**

And lastly, we will take a look at how the ancient philosophy and practice of yoga is remarkably suited to help us with each one of the above – which goes some way to explaining how it has become so popular in these rapidly changing times.

The first step to dismantling the barriers we erect to change is acknowledging their very existence. However, we must do this in a way that is non-judgemental. We need to stay detached. We need to observe the fact that our emotions or fears may be holding us back – but without berating ourselves for it. We need to develop the skill of observation – of ourselves. Observe how we react to change; observe ourselves progressing through the change curve – without criticism or judgement. This detachment will then enable us to do something about it.

We also need to treat ourselves in the same way as we would treat others if we were helping them to change – with understanding. Heaping scorn and criticism on yourself for erecting a change barrier will only deepen your resolve and strengthen the self-made psychological barricade.

Good leaders of change are empathetic; they are able to put themselves in the shoes of their employees; look at things from their perspective. The best change leaders help their people to want to change.

We need to be our own change leader. To help ourselves minimize and overcome a barrier to change, we need to treat ourselves with empathy and understanding. Go easy on ourselves. Give ourselves a break. Observe our reactions and seek to understand where they have come from – and why. Again, without judgement.

Once we have done that, we can look at these alleged barriers in a new light for we will be in the right frame of mind to overcome them.

CHAPTER FIFTEEN

Admitting denial

Denial does not solve the problem. Denial does not make the problem go away. Denial does not give us peace of mind, which is what we are really seeking when we engage in it.
Denial is a liar. It compounds the problem, because it keeps us from seeing a solution, and taking action to resolve it. BILL KORTENBACH[1]

Denial

Denial is such a strong obstacle for change that it deserves its own chapter. As we discussed in the last part, it is also a common, natural reaction when change is forced upon us. But sometimes we occupy this space for far too long. The need to change is staring us in the face; the future is approaching and we can see it coming but we just don't want to confront it. It is too uncomfortable. It is too real. It is too hard. So we kid ourselves.

Frankly, sometimes it is just easier to be an ostrich.

We have all done it and we have all seen people doing it. It is stultifying, unproductive, harmful… and completely normal.

Sometimes it is just easier to be an ostrich.

Denial is a common trait when it comes to addictions, failing marriages and abusive relationships. One partner prefers to deny evidence of infidelity rather than confront it. An abused wife clings on to the belief that 'he's a good man who loves me really'. Obese people can be in denial that their weight is harming them or that they can do anything about it.

Stockholm Syndrome is an extreme form of denial, where a victim of kidnapping starts to form a close affinity with their kidnappers – in complete denial of the situation in which they have found themselves.

We can even be in denial of our own medical conditions. One lovely lady I know with a history of high blood pressure was in such a strong state of denial that she refused to use the blood pressure testing kit the doctor had given her because she 'was fine'. When asked whether she had been using it, her response was 'Oh stop fussing!' She didn't even go to her GP for regular checkups because she didn't want to bother the doctor. 'I don't want to waste his time when it could be used for people who are really ill.' Even after the inevitable stroke, she apologized to the ambulance officers for bothering them. 'I feel like a bit of a fraud', she slurred as they were carrying her out on a stretcher into the waiting ambulance. (The good news is that two years on, she has made a full recovery and, allegedly, tests her blood pressure several times a week.)

I know of a young man who is beyond clinically obese. He is in his mid-thirties and is unlikely to work another day in his (probably shortened) life. He hasn't suffered any physical injuries. His legally recognized incapacity is entirely down to his weight. Why is he so obese? Well, logically that is easy. He eats far too much, especially far too much sugar and processed foods. He drinks too many sugary drinks and he drinks too much alcohol. In fact, he displays all the signs of being an alcoholic. And he gets no exercise. The repercussions of his obesity? His body is shutting down, his internal organs are struggling to cope, his legs and knees can't stand the strain and he is now very diabetic. He is jobless, hope-less and he gives all the appearance of someone who has given up on himself. He is in denial about his diet; in denial about his drinking; in denial about his lifestyle; and in denial that he can do anything about it. Surely, you can't get more of a 'burning platform' for change than that! Yet he does not possess the ability or the motivation to change. To him, this first change barrier is insurmountable and without overcoming his denial, he is unable to see the whole transformation through to its slimmer, healthier and happier conclusion.

Logically, this young man would rather be healthy, employed and live a longer life. But as we will discuss in the next section, even when the situation is dire, logic is insufficient. Logic won't fix him. Deeply rooted psychological barriers are preventing him from saving his own life. He lacks the emotional motivation to change.

But of course, denial comes in less dramatic forms as well – we all suffer from it on a daily basis. We kid ourselves that we have done enough work to do well in an exam. We deny that our credit card spending has got out of hand. We believe, without evidence, that we deserve the promotion we missed out on or the new contract we didn't win.

Sometimes our denial is well meaning. We don't want to insult our partner; we want to protect our loved ones. But in the end, we just don't want to face up to the truth because the truth can be messy and sometimes awfully difficult to deal with. Of course, more often than not, the longer we deny the truth, the harder it is to accept. I tell my corporate clients that when it comes to change, you either have to pay now or pay later – and it always costs far more when you pay later. It is the same for all of us.

Admitting denial

Admitting that you are in a state of denial is a really difficult, yet essential, first step to moving past it. Acknowledging that you have been kidding yourself is inordinately tough. We all kid ourselves from time to time; it is a normal human protection mechanism. But none of us likes to hear it, even from ourselves. Try it: tell yourself you are in a state of denial and watch what happens. Watch how you initially resist this criticism; how you deny your own state of denial. But simply by observing this, you will have planted a seed. Let it grow. When you are ready, you will come to see the world for what it is. But remember that denial is a very powerful state of inertia. Most politicians never recover from it – most likely because to recover from a state of denial you first have to admit you were wrong in the first place. This requires putting your ego to one side.

But once we do admit it, we can begin to look at the world afresh. If your previous image of what was happening wasn't real – what is?

CHAPTER SIXTEEN

Harnessing our emotions

Emotions can get in the way or get you
on the way. MAVIS MAZHURA[1]

Emotions

Our emotions are an incredibly strong barrier to change. Our emotions affect our decisions at the best of times, but when we are going through major change, our emotions can rule us. The way to lessen their impact is to observe them.

The first five steps of the Burning Platform Change Curve we discussed in the previous part – from Shock and Denial through to Anger, Fear and Depression – are all emotional. It isn't until Understanding that logic starts to kick in. But logic isn't enough, for emotion swiftly returns when our heart becomes engaged in the Acceptance stage.

Emotion is four times more powerful than logic. This startling fact was the conclusion of a 2004 study of some 50,000 employees by the US-based Corporate Leadership Council.[2] It concluded that, when it comes to engaging employees, emotional commitment is four times more powerful than rational commitment. The power of your emotions is not to be underestimated.

A change of status can unleash resistance to change

A change that many of my friends and colleagues are having to cope with at the moment is children leaving home. This change occurs every year in countless households across our nations. It is a change in the way the family used to be and can trigger a yearning for how things were. For many of us, it is also a change of status. A significant element of our identity as parent has just changed, to a profound degree, forever. To some parents, mostly but not exclusively mothers, it is not only a change of status but a loss of status, which can feel devastating. The fact it often occurs at the same time as the emotional and physical roller-coaster known as the menopause only serves to heighten the feeling of loss. For two decades, her status as the mother of children has been clear. And then one day, the nest is empty.

While this sort of loss of status can make us feel sad, losses of status at work can also make us angry. An organizational restructure where we end up reporting to someone else or our responsibility is diminished can even push us into The Trough.

We need to be treated fairly

If we sense that we have been treated unfairly, we get angry, and we resist the change. We humans need to believe that we have been treated fairly relative to others, that another group has not been favoured in some way. This is a strong resistor to accepting change. Which means it can also be a strong motivator for change as well! An obvious example springs to mind that acutely affected both the United States and the UK.

After decades of being ignored by politicians of all persuasions, the millions of people who had been left behind by globalization then found that they were the ones who were being forced to pay the price for the hubris and greed of the banking industry during the 2007–08 credit crisis. They paid for the banking collapse in the form of lower wages, unemployment, under-employment, loss of housing and lower standards of living. During the decade after the recession, the inequality gap between the top 1 per cent and the bottom 50 per cent increased even further as stock markets doubled and bankers' bonuses resumed as a result of the financial sleight-of-hand known as quantitative easing.

The inherent unfairness was a major cause of both Trump's election and Brexit. Voters were angry. They had been left behind and traditional politicians just didn't seem to care.

Once we become stuck in one of these emotional states, we can become trapped by our emotions and find it extraordinarily difficult to change. Sometimes, our emotions are so powerful that they can be overwhelming. And when it comes to significant change, they often will be. We have all been there. Shock can leave us stunned, unable to speak or move. 'Like a rabbit caught in the headlights.' Time seems to slow. Our blood pressure decreases. It can be as though we are having an out-of-body experience. Our emotions not only rule our decisions, they can control our bodies too. When this happens, we need help – either from within or from someone else who can help us understand what is happening, let us know it is normal and help us to see them for what they are.

Sometimes, our emotions are so powerful that they can be overwhelming.

Overcoming emotional states cannot be done by swimming against the tide. When you are caught in what Australians call a 'rip' (ie a powerful undertow that can sweep you out to sea, common to many surf beaches) you need to swim sideways across the flow. Accept you are being dragged out but know that if you swim perpendicular to the flow of water, you will eventually swim free of the rip. Too many people who swim against the rip end up exhausted and overwhelmed by the force of the ocean current. If they are not rescued in time, they drown.

How to harness our emotions

First, observe them

The first thing to do is to recognize them for what they are – emotional reactions to change that are completely normal and completely understandable. Take some time to simply observe them. The very nature of doing this will provide some space, some distance between you and the emotions you are observing. You can't be defined by them – they aren't you; they are separate things entirely. Fear doesn't define you. Anger doesn't define you, neither does 'Depression'. They are simply emotions. Observe them with curiosity and without judgement.

Of course you are experiencing fear – you wouldn't be human if you weren't worried about the implications of the change. Of course you are experiencing anger – it is a natural reaction to what has happened to you. Of course you are feeling sorry for yourself and even a tad depressed. These are all normal reactions. But also know that the next step will be upwards. Understanding is looking over the horizon. Help yourself prepare to emerge from The Change Curve by simply observing your emotions without judgement and without reacting to them.

Mindfulness teachers the world over recommend a simple but brilliant little mnemonic – the origin of which Deepak Chopra attributes to the current Dalai Lama:

STOP.

Stop. Take a breath. Observe. Proceed.

When confronted by anything that we perceive to be negative or challenging, he suggests that allowing ourselves the time and space simply to observe will make the world of difference.

Often things aren't as bad as they first appear or we have misunderstood the situation. Our emotions can turn us into a gunslinger – shooting first and asking questions later – when what we need to do is the very opposite. Stop, take a breath and observe before proceeding.

The next time I receive an email or tweet that makes me livid, I will try to remember this simple little technique – before letting them have it with both (considered) barrels!

Then, find your own emotional triggers

You have had change done to you. Don't wait for someone else to help – it may not be forthcoming. It's time to become your own therapist, which means harnessing your emotions to motivate yourself.

In order to be ready to work out the best course of events you should follow given the 'curve ball of change' that has been thrown your way, you first will need to engage yourself emotionally – to get yourself genuinely excited about the change. For if our excitement for the future is genuine, we have a damn good chance of making it happen. If our heart isn't in it – we don't.

You know yourself better than anyone.

You know how you react – which emotions come to the fore, when and why. You know which emotions motivate you. When it comes to change that has been done to you, you know precisely how you would like the other party to have made you feel. When it comes to change at work, you know what you wish the leaders had done, how they should have behaved and the assistance they should have provided. So now it's up to you to do it without them.

What gets you fired up? What gets you enthusiastic about the future? What makes you feel good about yourself? It's time to put *you* on the therapist's couch; it's time to psychoanalyse yourself. You need to work out what needs to be done to bring your best emotions into play.

Of course, you will almost certainly be your own worst critic, so whatever you decide to do must be genuine. Positive mental attitude is not enough. Few of us are narcissistic enough to be able to con ourselves – well, for long anyway. More than anyone else alive, we know deep inside when we are kidding ourselves – and it just won't work this time.

You've done your homework, now it's time to engage yourself emotionally. It's time to choose your attitude.

And finally, choose your attitude

> *If you don't like something, change it. If you can't change it, change your attitude.* MAYA ANGELOU[3]

There is a highly entertaining, enticing and yet so simple solution to customer service that a young customer service director introduced me to many years ago called 'Fish!' (www.fishphilosophy.com). It also works as a great piece of self-psychotherapy.

The thing I love most about Fish! is the simple mantra of 'Choose Your Attitude'.

Fish! is the story of a fish market stall in Seattle that outsold every other stall by a country mile. They sold the same fish as everyone else. They were in the same location as everyone else. The only difference was that their employees decided that they were in the customer enjoyment business. As one of the fish sellers explains – he gets up every morning and asks himself to 'choose his attitude'. He can choose either to let life get him down or he can choose to bounce out of bed and make every customer experience memorable.

The secret of their success is as simple as that – Choose Your Attitude. Look them up on YouTube or go to www.fishphilosophy.com.

The four simple pillars of the Fish Philosophy are:

Be There: Be emotionally present for people. It's a powerful message of respect that improves communication and strengthens relationships.

Play: Tap into your natural way of being creative, enthusiastic and having fun. Play is the spirit that drives the curious mind, as in 'Let's play with that idea!' You can bring this mindset to everything you do.

Often, we think we are powerless when it comes to unexpected change. We aren't.

Make Their Day: Find simple ways to serve or delight people in a meaningful, memorable way. It's about contributing to someone else's life – not because you want something, but because that's the person you want to be.

Choose Your Attitude: Take responsibility for how you respond to what life throws at you. Your choice affects others. Ask yourself: 'Is my attitude helping my team? Is it helping my customers? Is it helping me? Is it helping me to be the person I want to be?'

I think Fish! is fabulous.

It is exactly the same when it comes to change. We can choose how to react. We can stay angry, wallow in denial, succumb to fear and hunker down in the trough of depression – or we can choose our attitude and start to take control.

Often, we think we are powerless when it comes to unexpected change. We aren't.

At the very least we can choose our attitude – a simple act that will instantly place us firmly in the driver's seat.

CHAPTER SEVENTEEN

Confronting our fears

Nothing in life is to be feared, it is only to be understood.
Now is the time to understand more, so that
we may fear less. MARIE CURIE[1]

Fear

Fear is 'False Evidence Appearing Real'. It is the most crippling of the emotions we experience when it comes to change. In its extreme form it can, quite literally, be paralysing.

Fear is an evolutionary survival mechanism. It is heightened anxiety about what we think may happen in the future. A fear of snakes is ultimately a fear of being bitten by one. A fear of crocodiles is ultimately a fear of being eaten by one. I am not actually afraid of heights; I am afraid of falling from a great height. We aren't afraid of criticizing our boss per se, we are afraid of the consequences of criticizing our boss. In a very real sense, all fear is a fear of the future.

Being fearful of the future can cause people to anticipate bad things ahead and exaggerate both their likelihood and their importance. As Rosabeth Moss Kanter, Professor at Harvard Business School, said in the September 2012 *Harvard Business Review*, 'People will often prefer to remain mired in misery than to head toward the unknown'.[2]

The anticipation of something bad occurring makes us far more anxious than the certain knowledge that it will happen. This phenomenon was highlighted at Maastricht University in a well-known experiment that involved subjecting volunteer students to a succession of 20 electric shocks. Half of them were forewarned that they would receive 20 intense electric shocks. The other half were told they would receive 17 mild shocks and 3 intense shocks, but they didn't know when the intense shocks would occur. Those in group two sweated profusely and their heart rates were far higher than those in group one.

Fear of the future can be triggered by a loss of certainty. Being placed at risk of redundancy is an obvious version of this particular loss. It can trigger a fear of loss of status, loss of identity and/or a fear of financial insecurity. From the moment you receive that clunky, clinical letter, a blunt and cold feeling starts at the pit of your stomach and doesn't let up until some form of certainty has been restored. But 'loss of certainty' can also be more perception than reality. The perception of a change in the mood of a partner can also trigger feelings of uncertainty about the relationship, uncertainty about the future, even when nothing tangible has been said or done.

But while all fear may indeed be a form of 'fear of the future', it is obviously a multi-headed hydra, but the three main 'heads' of fear that are most pertinent to the world of change are:

1 Fear of failure (and its stranger cousin, fear of success).
2 Fear of blame.
3 Fear of the unknown.

Let's discuss each one in a little detail...

Fear #1: fear of failure

> *Failure seldom stops you. What stops you*
> *is the fear of failure.* JACK LEMMON[3]

Fear of failure, or 'atychiphobia' to give it its formal name, is one of the strongest sources of resistance to change. In business and in life, we humans are petrified of failing.

Atychiphobia can even manifest itself physically – shortness of breath, quickened heart rate, chest tightness, dizziness, indigestion... the same way that any form of anxiety or stress can affect us.

Sometimes we can be so afraid of failure that we feel that it is better not to try. We can end up handicapping ourselves so much that we bring about the very failure that we were so desperate to avoid in the first place

It is why most people don't quit their job and buy that bar in the Bahamas. It keeps us in a job we hate; in a loveless relationship.

We worry that we don't have the skills to compete in the new world – and that we don't have the aptitude to develop them.

Sometimes we can be so afraid of failure that we feel that it is better not to try.

We need to learn to strive for excellence but to expect failures along the way. Individuals who consistently fear failure tend to set goals that are too high or too low and become easily discouraged by obstacles.

FEAR OF SUCCESS?

Sometimes fear of failure is disguised as its weirder and most unexpected cousin – fear of success. To some of us, the thought of success can be just as scary. What if I am successful? How does that play against the story I have been telling myself all these years? What disruptive changes would success cause? What are the unintended consequences of success?

To me, this is just the flip side of the same coin. I brand both as fear of failure – as the key fear of succeeding is really a fear that future failure would then be even more dramatic. The successful have further to fall.

Fear of failure is a genuine and common barrier to change. But it is also one in which we must work to overcome – or we will never try to change anything.

OVERCOMING FEAR OF FAILURE

> *Forget about the consequences of failure. Failure is only a temporary change in direction to set you straight for your next success.* DENIS WAITLEY[4]

We all suffer from fear of failure. Actors suffer from it before every performance – they call it stage fright. We all experience butterflies before interviews, speeches and presentations; the bigger the occasion, the bigger the butterflies. It is normal and natural. The trick is not to let this fear become so large that it stops you dead in your tracks.

One way to do this is to put the change into perspective. Play Devil's Advocate. So what if it doesn't work out? What am I afraid of? What is the worst that could happen? These questions can help take the sting out of the fear.

Another tip is to take the future one step at a time. There's a reason why sports people often say they will be taking it 'one game at a time'. It breaks the actions down into controllable, bite-sized chunks and keeps the fear of failure at bay.

Thirdly, don't aim for perfection.

I gave a speech at an international conference a few years ago and I was petrified. It was so important to me to do a great job that the thought of not being absolutely perfect was quite literally unbearable. I took my script with me up to the lectern so that I wouldn't miss anything out and referred to it far too many times during the talk. When I sat down afterwards, I wanted the world to swallow me up. 'That was great!' declared the organizer I was seated next to. 'I thought it was the worst speech that I have ever given', I mumbled. 'Well', she said, turning to me. 'Only you and I know you can do even better than that. And everyone else thought it was brilliant.' I raised my eyes to find that a queue of smiling faces had formed behind me, wanting me to sign copies of *The Change Catalyst*. It appears that the speech was a success after all, but I was too focused on a futile quest for perfection to see it. The next time I gave that speech, I left the script in my briefcase and spoke from the heart. I left several parts out but the end result was immeasurably better.

And this time even I knew it.

EMBRACING FAILURE

But perhaps the best way to overcome fear of failure is to embrace it.

The unstoppable founder of Spanx, Sara Blakely, started her new hosiery business from her apartment in 2000 making pantyhose without seamed toes that didn't roll up her leg. Using US $5,000 of savings and an incredible amount of determination, Sara built a company worth more than US $1 billion.

She likes to describe how from a very early age her father used to invite her and her brother to share their failures at the family dinner table as they dined. Instead of being disappointed or upset, he would celebrate their efforts.

'What it did was reframe my definition of failure', Blakely said of the tradition. 'Failure for me became not trying.'[5]

'My dad would encourage me any time something didn't go the way I expected to write down where the hidden gifts were and what I got out of it', she said. 'I started realizing that in everything there was some amazing nugget that I wouldn't have wanted to pass up.'

Sara Blakely is one of the world's most successful entrepreneurs and in demand as a keynote speaker worldwide. Her fortune is built on embracing, and learning from, failure.

Fear #2: fear of blame

> *The urge to blame is based on the fear*
> *of being blamed.* DAVID STONE[6]

The fear of being blamed is a common source of change resistance in the workplace. If we have been responsible for doing things a certain way for some years, we fear that embracing a new way of working may be tantamount to admitting that we have been wrong all this time. We are afraid of being labelled as incompetent for not having changed earlier.

We fear that embracing a new way of working may be tantamount to admitting that we have been wrong all this time.

Let's face it, none of us like being told that we are doing a bad job – or could have been doing a better job or have become complacent. Quite rightly, we fear the consequences of such a revelation.

It's alright for the leadership to talk about 'continuous improvement' and 'innovation' but what happens if I can't see a way to improve the process for which I am responsible? What happens if I am not prone to innovative insights? I can tell you what will happen – I will be blamed for accepting or presiding over the current state of affairs. I will become the problem.

No-one wants that.

It is easy to spot someone suffering from a fear of being blamed, for they instantly go on the attack. When confronted by new ideas, they will lash out at the person suggesting the changes – directly and indirectly. They will tend to 'play the man and not the ball' to use a sporting analogy; working to discredit the harbinger of change as being inexperienced, unduly influenced by people with mal intent or swayed by people who don't know what they are talking about. The experience, competence and judgement of those suggesting the changes will be brought into question. As will their ideas. 'We looked at this years ago' is an oft-heard phrase from someone suffering from a fear of being blamed.

CASE STUDY: 'THE PRACTICE OF SHINING LIGHT'
The Plum Village Thai Buddhist Monastery has a unique way of encouraging their monks to accept accountability and provide feedback to their peers. As I mentioned in *The Change Catalyst*, each monk is asked to 'shine a light of their mindfulness on a situation':[7]

> At least once a year, every monk kneels down before his brothers and asks them to shine a light on him, meaning to tell him how they see him, to express themselves concerning his body, his feelings, his perceptions, his strengths and weaknesses. His brothers come together to provide him with the advice he needs. After having received the recommendations of his brothers, the monk prostrates deeply before them three times in thanks, and in the days that follow he tries to practice in the light of their recommendations.
>
> This kind of love letter from your Sangha (the Buddhist monastic community) can help you see clearly what you should and should not do; and you can do the same thing with your family, your parents, or your partner. You have a need for illumination and the other person does, too. So you can say to them, 'My dear one, you must help me. I have my strengths and weaknesses, and I want you to help me to see them more clearly. I have within me positive seeds, such as hope, understanding, compassion and joy, and I try to water them every day. I would like you to recognize the presence of these seeds in me and to try to water them several times a day, too. That will be a pleasure for me, and if I blossom like a flower, that will be a pleasure for you, too.
>
> For my part, I promise you that I will do my best to recognize and water the positive seeds in you, and I appreciate them a lot. Every time the seeds manifest, I am very happy, because at such times you are wonderful. You are so full of love and joy that I vow to water these seeds in you every day. I see as well that there are seeds of suffering in you, and I will make every effort not to water these. In that way I will not make you suffer, either'.

Can you imagine your leaders at work doing this? Humbly throwing themselves at the mercy of their peers and hoping beyond logic that it would end well.

But imagine the benefits if they did! The misunderstandings that would be dispelled; the clarity that would ensue; all those 'elephants in the room' that would become visible; the teamwork that would start to emerge based on humility, deep understanding and shared objectives.

Oh well. Let's get back to the real world.

OVERCOMING A FEAR OF BLAME: BECOME PART OF THE SOLUTION

You either have to be part of the solution, or you're going to be part of the problem. ELDRIDGE CLEAVER[8]

If the reason you are resisting change is because you are afraid that you may be blamed for the current way things are done – congratulations! Realizing this is your first step to a better future.

The next step is to openly embrace the new suggestions. Rather than focusing on how you can persuade everyone that the suggested change is wrong, agree that there is scope for improvement and help the person suggesting the change to focus on the outcomes they are trying to achieve and work back from there. Believe that the change agent in question is coming from a good place – to make the business work better. They won't have all the answers, neither do they have your experience. They need your help. Give it to them. Together, you could really make a difference.

Rise above any perceived criticism because it may not even exist.

In other words, rise above any perceived criticism because it may not even exist. You are bigger than this. No-one expects you to be perfect, neither do they expect you to have all the answers either. But they should expect you to continually look for improvements to the way you do things. Don't be a saboteur. Be part of the solution – willingly. Because if you are not part of the solution... well, you are part of the problem. If you actively resist change, this is how others will see you.

That is unlikely to end well.

Fear #3: fear of the unknown

*The oldest and strongest emotion of mankind
is fear, and the oldest and strongest kind of fear
is fear of the unknown.* H P LOVECRAFT[9]

Fear of the unknown is so important and so prevalent that many psychologists declare it to be 'the fundamental fear' that underlies anxiety and neuroticism.

It is, by definition, an uncertain threat. But it is more than simply worrying about something that hasn't happened or may not happen. It is literally fear of something we don't know; fearing something we don't understand or something that may not even happen. It is unpredictable in its timing, intensity, frequency or duration and elicits a generalized feeling of apprehension and hypervigilance.

At one level it can be what psychologists call 'anticipatory anxiety'. Anxiety about pending pain can sometimes be more painful than the actual pain.

At the next level it can manifest itself as an anxiety that something bad may happen. This anxiety can be physical, causing breathlessness, a feeling of being trapped and a racing heart beat as we play and replay the worst case scenarios in our head. We are experiencing the bad event yet we don't even know if it is going to occur. Of course, 99 per cent of the time, it doesn't. As my father once said, 'Don't tell me that worrying doesn't help. Everything I worry about doesn't happen!'

At its extreme, this fear can lead to an anxiousness about things we can't even imagine. It's the 'unknown unknowns' these extreme sufferers worry about.

But it's the milder form of this fear that we should focus on here – fear of the 'known unknowns'. It is fear of what lies ahead, especially when we are embarking on something new. It is fear of the type of people we may find in the new neighbourhood. It is fear of starting your own business when you have no idea how! It is fear of moving into the new team at work. It is aligned to the fear of failure, but it is different. We can overcome our fear of the unknown – and still worry about not failing in the new world.

Fear of the unknown is a phenomenon that tends to increase with age. Children take to new technology without missing a beat. Teenagers across our nations are the first to be asked to 'fix the TV' or 'do something about the wifi'. Older people, in the main, tend to be more fearful of the unknown – from new technology to social change to foreigners.

It is also an in-built evolutionary response. For survival purposes, we are hard-wired to be wary of what we don't know or understand.

OVERCOMING FEAR OF THE UNKNOWN
Knowledge is power. SIR FRANCIS BACON[10]

At its extremes, fear of the unknown can be dangerous. It is also completely normal. We all experience it. In fact, we wouldn't be human if we didn't.

To overcome our fear of the unknown, we need to make the unknown familiar.

For survival purposes, we are hard-wired to be wary of what we don't know or understand.

On the one hand, the Brexit vote in the UK displayed an admirable lack of fear of the unknown – for the list of known unknowns of Britain leaving the EU could fill a library! But 17.4 million people ticked the Leave box confident in Britain's ability to strike new trade deals with the world and thrive outside of the EU. For others, it was a vote for the unknown for the simple reason that they had nothing to lose.

For many, it was actually a rejection of change. It was a vote for a return to a known past. Some 33 per cent of those who voted Leave in the UK's 2016 EU referendum cited immigration as the primary reason for their choice.[11] Interestingly, there was a significant inverse correlation between the Leave vote and numbers of immigrants in the electorate – the more immigrants, the lower the vote to Leave. Places with more immigrants tended to vote Remain. Familiarity can breed contempt. It can also breed understanding.

When it comes to overcoming a fear of the unknown, a mindfulness technique is particularly relevant and useful.

Mindfulness teaches us to be still mentally by helping us to become aware of what our mind is doing. Not critical of it, just aware. It eases anxiety and mental stress and even helps with depression.

World-renowned Mindfulness Master, the ever-smiling Mingyur Rinpoche,[12] tells a story of how his father introduced him to the world of meditation and mindfulness. Young Mingyur suffered from constant fear of the unknown. He would experience severe panic attacks about storms and all sorts of events beyond his control. His father taught him how to meditate, starting with focusing on his breath and then eventually moving on to observe his thoughts and fears.

Three decades of meditation later and Mingyur tells us how he has learnt to face his panic: 'Don't fight with the panic. You have to say welcome to the panic. I'm not going to get rid of my panic. I use my panic, I watch my panic. I say, "Hello panic, welcome". So in the end me and my panic become good friends.'[13]

Note the lack of judgement. Mingyur doesn't think he is weak because he panics. His panic is a part of him. He can't get rid of it, so he doesn't try. He takes a completely different approach. Fighting our fears, or ignoring them, only fuels them. Acknowledging them deprives them of fuel. Befriending them weakens them.

If it is starting your own business you are worried about, do some research about how to do this. Speak to others who have done it recently and ask them what they would do differently next time.

If learning a new skill concerns you, explore how this could be done. It will not be as daunting as you may first think. It may even be the best thing you have done in your life.

Find out as much as you possibly can about the potential implications of the change before setting off. But in the end, no plan is perfect. So satisfy yourself as much as you can, gird your loins – and take the leap.

While there are obvious limits to tolerance and acceptance, if we wish to minimize the fear of the unknown, we need to make the unknown familiar.

CHAPTER EIGHTEEN

Finding good tribes

Belonging is our blessing, tribalism is our burden. DR SAUL LEVINE[1]

Our need to belong can lead to a mistrust, even fear, of others

We are a social species. We have evolved the need, and the skills, to form social groups for our protection and future prosperity. Our forager and hunter ancestors soon learnt the benefits of collaboration. We like to belong; we need to belong. Being part of a club, a clique, a group not only helps us to feel safe and secure, it even reinforces our own sense of identity. Belonging is a critical factor in our health and wellbeing.

But it also has its downsides. Our ancestors also learnt to be wary of 'others' and to this day, we are innately tribal; prone to quickly form gangs of 'us vs them'. Interestingly, a prerequisite for membership of any gang is that we must conform to the myths and mistruths that underline the group's core beliefs. Just look at the very human concept of nations. As citizens, we pride ourselves in our national identity and the myths and stories that go along with them. Citizens of other nations will look at our nation through a completely different lens. Their view of our nation may bear no resemblance to ours. Meanwhile they tell themselves their own stories about their own national identity and values, which we may think are equally preposterous.

Of course, this does not only apply to nations. The same is true for any groups to which we belong – political, religious, social.

Another fascinating observation about human behaviour is that our need to belong is so strong that we will not only accept the myths and mistruths that our group propagates, but we will also simply dismiss facts that fly in the face of our group's core beliefs. It is simply too important that we belong – for our own self-esteem, for our mental health and for our sense of security. There is safety in numbers.

We see this with any political group. President Trump's most ardent followers are an ideal example. Even the most brazen of his lies and most objectionable of his comments are either believed to be fabricated by his opponents or simply discarded as irrelevant – or both. If another politician were to refer to themselves as a 'stable genius', or tell non-white Congresswomen to 'go back to where you came from', or allegedly obstruct justice, or fight so vehemently not to publish their tax returns, or praise murderous dictators, or declare that non-European immigration is to blame for US troubles, or to cancel a state visit to Denmark because they wouldn't sell Greenland to him, or try to extort foreign leaders into conducting enquiries into their political opponents, or pretend that tariffs on Chinese goods were a tax that China paid... his supporters would be outraged. Believing him, even when he is contorting the truth; agreeing with him, even when he is taking a wrecking ball to the rule of law and free press; discounting his 'alleged' negatives – are all part of the rights and responsibilities of membership to the Pro-Trump club.

The rise of White Supremacist and Neo-Nazi groups across the United States and the world is another frightening example of this phenomenon. The pitiful and misogynistic men (and the pitiful and self-loathing women who stick by their White Supremacist partners) who join these horrific groups are full to the brim with hate – for society, for liberals, for 'elites', for LBGT+ people, for educated women – for anyone whom they can attempt to blame for the fact that they have been left behind both economically and socially. Their jobs have disappeared, their self-esteem has evaporated and their hope left them long ago. Even their stereotypical view of what it means to be a man is now regarded by the rest of society as Neanderthal. They are lost and they are angry. Their self-loathing is being channelled into a violent hatred of people who are not like them. And of course, the easiest way to determine people who are not like you is skin colour.

But we don't have to search for extremes to see fear of others in action. We see it in virtually every instance we gather together and form a group – every clique, every club, every religion, every sect, every political party, every business, and often even departments within businesses.

Every business tells itself that it is better than the competition. But we form tribes within our company as well – Sales v Marketing, Sales v Service, Propositions v Operations, Finance v Everyone... Whenever we take a person out of one team and place them into another, their immediate reaction is often to start seeing what is wrong with their previous team. We need to be constantly on the lookout for instances where we are 'going tribal'; forming cliques that only serve to criticize others and dampen any opposing views. In business, that way leads to silos. In society, it can be even more dangerous.

Whenever we take a person out of one team and place them into another, their immediate reaction is often to start seeing what is wrong with their previous team.

Social media exacerbates our innate tribalism; trapping us in an echo chamber, a self-serving bubble where we only see like-minded viewpoints. We now form new tribes online – and those tribes attack one another mercilessly. The raw hatred unleashed on Twitter can be truly frightening.

Politicians have always played upon our evolutionary tribalism; our inbuilt wariness of 'others'. They still do today and we seem to fall for it every time. One would think that by now modern humans would be immune to this sort of manipulation; that with the documented knowledge and understanding we have of countless historical lies and the countless atrocities that have been committed in the name of exceptionalism and nationalism, we would understand the dangers of xenophobia. But we don't. We still allow politicians to manipulate us, to play upon these ancient, evolutionary fears – even though the logical part of our brain knows that this is likely to have disastrous consequences. We just can't seem to help it.

One of the most assured ways of getting elected, even today, is to unite a proportion of the population against a common foe – perceived or real. Often perceived. When it came to declaring war on Iraq, George W Bush galvanized his patriotic followers with the phrase, 'You are either with us or against us'. During Gulf War II, a majority of Americans believed that Iraq had played a part in 9/11 and 'Dubya' let this lie persist, as it served his purposes. He even identified an 'Axis of Evil' that the United States and its allies (evidently on the side of the angels!) should fight against. The latest US President has since refined the 'Axis of Evil' to an axis of one: Iran. Meanwhile the Iranian Ayatollahs paint the United States as 'The Great Satan'.

As an integral part of his successful 2016 election campaign, Donald Trump stoked the embers of xenophobia – attacking Muslims, Mexicans and anyone who was an 'other' in the eyes of his core supporters. And he hasn't stopped since. In fact, appealing to his electorate's insular fear of others and continuing to wrap this xenophobia in the US flag is such a powerful ploy that it may see him re-elected in November 2020. And this is precisely how 2020 began – with the assassination of a high-profile Iranian General on the streets of Iraq via a US military drone strike, the reassignment of thousands of additional US troops to the Middle East (having previously sworn to pull the United States out of the region) and then tweeting images of Congress Democrats in Muslim attire, claiming that they would rather side with Iran than the United States. The truly depressing thing is that it works.

In the UK, immigration was a key reason behind a significant proportion of the 2016 Leave vote. Obviously being concerned about immigration does not make you a xenophobe – far from it. But a number of people were prompted to vote Leave by xenophobic rhetoric. Brazenly racist acts have increased across the UK since the referendum.

At least a third of Leave voters were willing to give up their own freedom of movement across Europe if it meant the ability to curb immigration into Britain.

In a double dose of irony, much of the UK electorate didn't understand that, within EU laws, it already had the power to restrict immigration anyway.

'As a rule, strong feelings about issues do NOT emerge from deep understanding.'[2]

As I am writing this book, Austria's governing coalition is effectively being ruled by the far right 'Freedom Party of Austria'. Germany's 'Alternative for Germany' has 94 seats in the German Bundestag, and Spain's far right Vox party now holds 15 per cent of the seats in a hung parliament and has become a major force in Spanish politics. Hungary's Prime Minister Orban was re-elected in 2018 in no small measure by demonizing Jews in general and George Soros in particular. Many world commentators describe Orban's government to be dictatorial and autocratic. Naturally, the current US President has praised Orban's hard-line approach.

Seventy-five years since the end of the Second World War, we seem to have forgotten the devastating danger of giving in to xenophobia.

As a supposedly intelligent species, we shouldn't tolerate this.

Tolerance is wrong

The best and worst of human nature are on display every minute of the day on Twitter. Ever since the EU referendum, the British Twittersphere has been brimming with stories of EU citizens being refused the right to remain in Britain even though they have lived in the country for decades. Stories abound of the verbal abuse of foreign-born doctors, nurses, shopkeepers and everyday citizens. International post-grad students have been asked to leave. During one such online exchange, a born-and-bred British National reacted to this travesty with the comment: 'If you weren't born here, you have no right to remain here. We tolerate you. That doesn't mean we accept you.'

Sometimes my fellow humans make me want to weep.

Other people are just that – people. They have the same hopes, dreams and fears as you do; as I do. Often, if we treat them how we would like to be treated if we were in their position, we would be amazed at the response. We need to spend more time focusing on the things we have in common and celebrate the differences. If their religious practices and social norms aren't harming us, how about we simply accept them? Just because they are different doesn't mean they are inferior – or dangerous. Even the most alien of cultures have a few redeeming features!

We need to spend more time focusing on the things we have in common and celebrate the differences.

The United States, Canada, UK, Australia, New Zealand, Europe... we like to pride ourselves on being 'tolerant' societies: tolerant of different religions; tolerant of different sexual orientations; tolerant of different cultures; tolerant of different people. I have always been proud to be a citizen of countries that are tolerant. But I was wrong. It wasn't until I lived in Abu Dhabi for a few years and I was the one who felt 'tolerated' that I realized that 'tolerance' is not enough.

The UAE is rightly proud of its tolerance, especially its religious toler-ance. They have a government Minister of Tolerance and declared 2019 to be 'The Year of Tolerance'. Shiites are tolerated. Non-Muslims are tolerated. Christians are tolerated. Mormons are tolerated (although a few I know were once asked to stop knocking on doors trying to convert locals to their faith…). Western drinking habits are tolerated. Western people eating pork is tolerated. Western women wearing skimpy bathing costumes around hotel pools is tolerated. Innumerable other 'vices' are also tolerated – or at least ignored. Even holding hands in public is frowned upon but tolerated – as long as you are married or, ironically, of the same gender.

In 2019, Pope Francis became the first Pope to visit the Middle East and he held a Catholic mass in Abu Dhabi's Zayed Sports Stadium for 120,000 ex-pat Catholics (mainly from The Philippines and India). The Pontiff was embraced publicly by The Grand Imam of al-Azhar, the spiritual leader of Sunni Islam. I openly and wholeheartedly applaud The Grand Imam and the leaders of the UAE for doing this. It is a grand gesture and a meaningful and significant step in the right direction. Christians weren't just tolerated – they were accepted. The global leader of the largest Christian church was publicly embraced and treated as an equal. It was a very public display of acceptance and change.

Tolerance implies reluctance; it suggests superiority. I tolerate your actions and beliefs.

The day after Pope Francis's mass, a man was jailed for wearing a Qatar football shirt.

While living in the Middle East, I had an epiphany of sorts: None of us want to be tolerated. We want to be accepted. 'Tolerance' implies reluctance; it suggests superiority. 'I *tolerate* your actions and beliefs.'

We all need to move beyond 'tolerance'; we need to accept other people. 'Acceptance' is far healthier; for acceptance requires understanding. Acceptance requires an appreciation of differences. Acceptance implies equality. The Grand Imam, who is from Egypt, hit it on the head the year before the Pontiff's first Middle Eastern mass when he declared that, 'Christians should not call themselves a minority; they are citizens like anyone else'. This statement implies something more than tolerance. It implies acceptance.

It made me realize that in the West we too 'tolerate' a number of people and practices that are different from our cultural norms. And we shouldn't. 'Tolerance' is simply not good enough. We need to accept them.

However... there are certain behaviours that we should not accept. We shouldn't accept discrimination, racism, hate speech or misogyny from any member of our society – even locals. Actually – especially locals. We shouldn't accept habitual lying from our politicians. We shouldn't accept tax dodging from multinational companies. We certainly shouldn't *tolerate* any of this – yet we do.

Our lack of clarity around cultural norms could be a major fuel for xenophobia and racism and one of the causes of the current populist political backlash we see across the West. Because we don't state the values of our society clearly, we end up 'tolerating' all sorts of behaviours that we shouldn't – from existing citizens and newcomers alike. What does it mean to be British? What does it mean to be American? What does it mean to be Australian? Canadian? New Zealand? Finnish? French? Italian? Indian?...

The rights of citizenship should come with a corresponding set of responsibilities. Yet we don't seem to spell these out. What are the attitudes and codes of behaviour that the nation expects in return for the gift of citizenship? And citizenship *is* a gift. Strangely, it is a gift that is often valued more highly by people who have chosen to become citizens compared to those who were accidentally born in the country.

New Zealand's magnificent and, frankly, incomparable Prime Minister, Jacinda Ardern, obviously agrees. In the immediate aftermath of the horrific terrorist mass shooting of innocent worshippers in two mosques by a White Supremacist in Christchurch in March of 2019, she quickly condemned both him and his ideology: 'It is clear that this can now only be described as a terrorist attack', the PM said. She went on to say that New Zealand was targeted because it 'represents the values of diversity, kindness and compassion':

> We are home for those who share our values and a refuge for those who need it. And those values I can assure you will not and cannot be shaken by this attack...
>
> We are a proud nation with more than 200 ethnicities and 160 languages and amongst the diversity that we share common values and the one that we place currency on right now is our compassion, and our support for

the community of those directly affected by this tragedy. And secondly, the strongest possible condemnation of the ideology of the people who did this. You may have chosen us but we utterly reject and condemn you.

Find good tribes

'Other people matter.'[3]

Much of human behaviour, thought and emotion stems from our psychological need to belong. The emotional consequences of belonging have been well studied. A strong sense of belonging is a major cause of greater self-esteem, happiness and wellbeing. It also acts as a buffer against stress and a protection against depression. Social connections are so important that in 2011, the US Centers for Disease Control and Prevention (CDC) adopted 'promoting connectedness' as its core strategic direction for preventing suicidal behaviour. Belonging prevents suicide.

Recognition from your peers is the most powerful form of recognition there is.

Among students, a sense of belonging to peers and teachers has been shown to be a key enabler of higher exam results.

In the work place, belonging to co-workers is often a better motivator than money. Recognition from your peers is the most powerful form of recognition there is. Neuroscientists have even proven this to be true – our brain's circuitry responds as strongly to social rewards (eg peer recognition) as it does to financial rewards. Belonging can also create meaning; being a part of a group means we are part of something larger than ourselves.

But the reverse is also true. When social ties are severed, our brains react as if we have been physically injured. We are wired to feel pain when bereft of social connection in much the same way as when we are hungry and thirsty.

Our need to belong is a strong and fundamental human need. So strong that it can lead us astray. It is why kids join gangs. It is how gang leaders are able to groom kids so easily into running drugs for them. It is why leaders of religious sects throughout the ages have been able to attract multitudes of people to join their self-destructive and pernicious clubs.

We need to find good tribes to join. I have often heard it said that there are two types of people in the world – energy givers and energy takers (or drains and radiators, if you prefer). We need to surround ourselves with radiators; with people who are energy givers. Life's too short for drains.

Take a step back and assess your own tribes. Do they reinforce your own personal values? Do they ignite the best parts of you? Do they accept the real you, warts and all? Do they make you feel like a better person? Are they energy givers or energy takers? Are you a 'drain' when in their company or are you a 'radiator'? Are they good for you?

Does your 'gang' at work give you energy or do they sap it from you? Are they incessantly complaining or do they also get around to trying to make things better? Are they wallowing in their cynical victimhood or are they reinforcing one another with belief and confidence? Now, I love a good dose of cynical victimhood as much as the next person (you should see some of my Twitter feed!) and let's face it, where would British and Australian humour be without cynicism and irony? But there comes a time when even I know this is counter-productive and it is time to lift my head and start to look for ways to get on the front foot, to be proactive, to change my attitude and make a difference. That may mean changing my tribes.

We can change our tribes. We have the power to do this.

Make sure your tribes are good for you.

CHAPTER NINETEEN

Reframing our identity

We are reduced to asking others what we are. We never dare to ask ourselves. JEAN-JACQUES ROUSSEAU[1]

Identity

Our view of who we are, the sort of person we are, the sort of decisions we make, the way we make decisions, the values we espouse, what we stand for and the sort of person we wish to be in the future... can all get in the way of embracing change.

We humans are complex beings and as we have seen, our mind controls our actions, effectively dictating what we can and cannot accomplish. And an incredibly strong part of our mind is wrapped up in our identity – who we think we are.

How do you see yourself? How would you describe yourself? Would you say you were a 'kind' person? Driven? Ambitious? Caring? Dutiful? Clever? Glamorous? Strong? Is your work an important part of your identity? Is your role as a mother or father or son or daughter an important part of who you are? Which values are key to your identity? Fairness? Entitlement? Exceptionalism? Which affiliations are important to you that they part-define who you are? Church? Mosque? Club? Political party?

Our identity is shaped by a plethora of external influences – our parents, our upbringing, our religion or lack of it, our ethnicity and the society in which we live. It is shaped by how we perceive what others think of us. Our nationality, or rather the values and philosophies we attribute to our nationality, can also play an important role in forging our identity, our attitudes and, in turn, our behaviours.

Our need to belong is an important part of our identity. We are social animals; our need to be part of social groups is an integral part of our evolutionary make-up. It is vital for our physical survival and our mental wellbeing. As we have discussed previously, our need to belong can be so strong that we are capable of performing all sorts of extraordinary mental gymnastics; dismissing truths and believing all sorts of myths just to remain part of the group.

Our need to belong is an important part of our identity.

Religious cults are another obvious example of this phenomenon. Being a member of the cult becomes so important to the identity of the cult's followers that they will endure no end of self-sacrifice and self-harm to maintain their membership. Countless documentaries have been made of how movements such as the Rajneeshis and Scientology were/are able to influence/brainwash their followers to such an extent that their sense of self was inseparable from membership of the cult.

On 19 November 1978, Reverend Jim Jones of The Peoples Temple Agricultural Project, better known as 'Jonestown', convinced his 900+ devoted followers to commit mass suicide by drinking Kool-Aid laced with cyanide. I can't even remember the cause that they died for. But died they did. A third of the dead were minors who were given the poison by their parents. The need to belong to this group was so strong that they killed their children and then themselves to maintain their membership, to maintain their identity.

Of course, our need for belonging can also be a force for good. Helping the needy is a core tenet of Christianity, Islam and the vast majority of religions. It is the basis of a large number of faith-based charities around the world. Our sense of identity can be an incredibly powerful driver of change.

It can also be an incredibly powerful barrier to change. Sometimes, in times of change, our need to adopt a new course of action comes head to head with our identity – and we can falter.

If 'resilience' is a key part of our identity, this may prevent us from calling an end to a negative relationship or a job that is not right for us. If 'I'm not

146

a quitter', is an important part of how we see ourselves, we are likely to persevere with a damaging situation far longer than we should.

If 'stoicism' is an important part of our identity, we may postpone visiting or calling the doctor, a delay that could potentially have disastrous consequences. And, of course, if our identity has become synonymous with 'victimhood', we will wallow in the trough of the Change Curve for far too long – perhaps forever.

Reframe our identity

Our identity is not set in stone. It is not 'final'. We can amend it. When the need to change clashes with the way we see ourselves, especially if the change clashes with our core beliefs and values, the barrier to change is extremely challenging.

It presents us with an opportunity to review how we see ourselves. It is an opportunity to review:

- what we stand for;
- who we choose to stand with;
- what we believe about ourselves;
- how we want to be seen – by ourselves and others – in the future;
- why.

Is your identity getting in the way of embracing this change? Are your 'values' clashing with the values you believe will be necessary to go along with this change? If the answer to either of these questions is yes, you will have one last question to answer: How important to you is the need to embrace this change?

If you judge it to be important enough then you will need to look at those elements of your identity that may need a little revision. You may need to reframe how you see yourself. You can still be 'stoic' but not to the point of never going to the doctor. You can still be a 'completer–finisher' while also being able to announce when a project cannot be delivered to its original deadline.

Our identity is not necessarily set in stone. Like our thoughts and our beliefs, it is malleable. But any change of identity we instigate must be genuine.

CHAPTER TWENTY

Testing our doubts

*The whole problem with the world is that fools and fanatics
are always so certain of themselves but wiser people
are so full of doubts.* BERTRAND RUSSELL[1]

Doubts

We all have doubts during any period of change. So we should. No change
is perfect. It's messy. It's complicated. The vision of the future that we had in
our heads rarely comes to fruition in the way that we originally envisioned.

This is true of almost any significant change – new relationships, new
jobs, new schools – no matter whether we have instigated it or whether it
has been forced upon us.

Of course, we see it at work all the time. The leader stands up and paints
a glorious vision of a new world of growth and opportunity for all – and as
we sit in the auditorium, we start to wonder. We wonder whether the boss's
forecast for the future is achievable. We wonder about the reasons behind
the change: they are telling us the 'right' reason but what is the 'real' reason?
We can see so many obstacles and they haven't even acknowledged them in
their 'motivational' speech! Doubt starts to creep in. A wonderful US CEO
described it to me from his perspective as: 'Cam, sometimes, they're just not
buyin' what I'm sellin'!'

This particular change barrier is more than fear of the unknown; it is full-blown scepticism about the stated benefits that the change will bring. It is not only an issue of belief; it is an issue of trust.

> *I do not trust that the future will be better than today. The Powers That Be may try to convince me that the numbers add up and the new structure will work better than the old one – but I am yet to be convinced. I query the figures, the assumptions, the assertions, the conclusions and the real reasons behind this change. I especially question your assertion that the results of the change will be good – for the company, for my colleagues or for me.*

When it comes to organizational change, these sorts of doubts are very common, but openly airing them can more often than not be a risky move! So before you decide to air them, take a deep breath and ask yourself the following pointed question.

What is it about the post-change vision of the future that your change leaders are promoting that you don't believe?

And why?

(A little side note about the related phenomenon of 'change fatigue'. It is a common ailment in companies that put their poor employees through one change programme after another. Many of the participants in my 'Leading Change' and 'Embracing Change' workshops describe 'change fatigue' as a major obstacle to change within their organizations. So many have told me this that I now include 'Treating change like a programme' as the 11th reason why corporate change fails. Change isn't a programme. It is constant. It's part of life. But to ingrain change into the culture of an organization, leaders need to vary the pace of change – no-one can keep going flat out!)

Test your doubts

Doubts are healthy. But we must do something with them or they fester and prevent us from action.

The first thing to do, as with any barrier to change, is acknowledge their existence – to air them. But please do this constructively! Perhaps start by airing them to yourself. I mean, if you have doubts over a new relationship, barging in and giving your partner a full serve of half-baked concerns without prior thought may be something you live to regret!

But when you have thought them through, definitely share them – in a way that is not accusatory or patronizing; in a manner that starts a conversation rather than ending one. And remember, the reason you are sharing these doubts is to test them. Accept they may be unfounded. They may not be as worrying as you imagine; or they may be right on the money. The only way to know is to submit them to closer inspection; to check how valid they may be. You may be pleasantly surprised or you may have uncovered a key reason why the change needs revising.

In the business example above, if you genuinely do not believe that the change that your organization's leaders are planning will make things better, try to do something about it. For as Leonardo Da Vinci once said, 'Nothing strengthens authority as much as silence'.

Seek to understand why the people instigating the change think it will bring about a brighter future.

But before you don your armour and march into battle, first seek to understand why the people instigating the change think it will bring about a brighter future. Try to take all of your biases and preconceptions and lock them in a box awhile. Then, wide-eyed and innocent, jump into giving them the benefit of the doubt and seek to comprehend the rationale and the vision that you have been sold. Then voice your doubts and start to test them.

If at the end of all this doubt-testing you still remain unconvinced, ask yourself two questions – and be painfully honest with your answers:

1 Is this a battle worth fighting?
2 Is it going to happen anyway, no matter what I do?

If your honest answer to the last question is yes, don't waste your time tilting at windmills – accept the reality and look for the opportunities.

The Serenity Prayer:

Grant me the serenity to accept the things I cannot change
the courage to change the things I can,
and the wisdom to know the difference.[2]

Detaching from our negative thoughts

*We are the products of the stories we
tell ourselves.* DERREN BROWN[1]

Negative thoughts

The human mind has somewhere between 50,000 and 80,000 thoughts
every day. And it is estimated that around 80 per cent of them are negative.
Our minds are continually trying to protect us and yet they are also apply-
ing the most insidious of brakes on future progress and change.

Imagine if those negative thoughts inside our head were an actual person;
someone who was always by our side, constantly looking for the negatives
in others; continually warning us to be wary of people whom this person
deems to be 'different' and reinforcing our evolutionary tribal instincts.
Constantly reminding us why we shouldn't do something; preaching that
we aren't worthy; urging us not to try because we might fail; telling us that
we didn't have the skills and we simply aren't good enough.

Why on earth would we keep hanging around with such a horrible
prophet of doom? Pretty soon, we would disassociate ourselves from them.
We would realize that they are talking nonsense and holding us back. We
would stop taking notice of them.

That 'person' is inside our heads – and they need taming if we wish to fulfil our true potential; if we wish to be happy and content; if we wish to change. We need to calm the almost constant din of negativity.

For our thoughts, if left unchecked, can be the biggest barriers to change of all.

Thoughts lead to feelings. Feelings lead to action and our actions affect how people react to us. Let me give you an example. A stranger walks into a pub and because of the way he looks, the way he is dressed, the way he sounds, you instantly think, 'He is nothing like me. I am not sure I like him and I don't think he will like me very much'. These thoughts produce feelings of wariness that guide your body language and your actions towards him. You may give him a wide berth, avoid his gaze or give him one of your best fake smiles. Without saying anything, he instantly gets the message and reacts accordingly. His barriers go up and he reacts in a similar fashion. Nothing has been said and yet these two strangers are already in confrontational mode.

Our thoughts, if left unchecked, can be the biggest barriers to change of all.

Imagine what would have happened if you had started with a different thought. The same stranger walks in and you think, 'Cool tattoos. I wonder where he had them done', or 'I bet he has a story or two!' These thoughts would generate positive feelings and perhaps even a natural smile – and he would react in turn. Nothing has changed but your thoughts – yet the world is suddenly a very different place.

Of course, this doesn't only pertain to chatting up bikers in bars. Your thoughts will guide the nature of every interaction in the same manner – with friends, work colleagues, relatives… Your thoughts – which are a product of your own biases, preconceptions and prejudices – will determine how you feel, which in turn drives how you act, which produces corresponding reactions in others.

Beliefs are another order of magnitude altogether; they are thoughts on steroids. A belief is a thought that we have started to make real, that we have begun to strengthen in our minds. If we are not careful, beliefs can become hard truths. In fact, we seem to be hard-wired to do just that.

We humans have a tendency to look for data and facts that support our beliefs, which in turn serves to harden them. Social media feeds upon this incessantly reinforcing our prejudices daily by showing us more of what it thinks we want to see. Unless we actively seek to follow people with contrarian views to our own, we end up trapped in an 'echo chamber' in which we only hear the opinions of people who share our views. We become increasingly convinced of our own rightness and righteousness. This is not only insular; it can be dangerous.

The internet was supposed to herald a new age of truth; the democratization of information. When facts were available to all, the truth would win out, banishing propaganda and mistruths forever. 'Sunlight is said to be the best of disinfectants', said Louis Brandeis.[2]

The predictions could not have been more wrong. The deluge of information online has made it almost impossible to distinguish truth from propaganda; fact from fiction; news from opinion; truth from lies. It has not only provided fertile ground for mistruths to flourish, it has provided corporations and governments with the tools to manipulate people in a manner that Goebbels would have killed for.

Our opinions are strengthened at every interaction with our online echo-chambers, playing on our evolutionary need to belong with the result that we seem to be becoming even more tribal with every passing click.

Today, we seem to define ourselves in deeply partisan ways – as Pro-Trump or Anti-Trump, Pro-Brexit or Anti-Brexit, Climate Change Sceptics or Followers of Science. Political discourse in the West has always been tribal, but it seems to have tipped over into hatred and loathing of the other side. We no longer simply disagree with the arguments emanating from our political opponents; we believe fervently that they are morally wrong and intellectually inferior. Our thoughts and opinions have not only been transformed into beliefs, they have been strengthened to the point of fanaticism; they have become visceral truths. And they have become personal.

We seem to be revelling in our beliefs and hardening our positions to such a degree that we are unable to listen, unable to even begin to see any credence in what the other side may be saying, because in our modern polarized world, acknowledging that your opponent may have made even a single point you agree with is tantamount to complete capitulation.

But then, sometimes we forget that this has been happening for thousands of years before social media. Mankind has been turning thoughts into beliefs, beliefs into 'hard truths' and 'hard truths' into disastrous action for millennia. Out of ignorance and politically induced fear, often fuelled by religious dogma, our ancestors have drowned 'witches', imprisoned scientists such as Galileo for daring to show that the Earth revolved around the Sun and embarked upon murderous crusades to conquer the Saracens or to kill the infidels.

Each of our religions lays claim to ownership of 'the truth' and beliefs swiftly become 'truth' in the eyes of the true believer, often with deadly consequences.

When followers of one religion genuinely believe that the word of (their) God, as written in their Holy texts, is 'the truth', they obviously also believe that followers of another religion and followers of no religion are therefore ignorant of, or perhaps even in denial of, 'the truth'. On its own, this belief is benign. But we know it hasn't always stopped there. Hardened beliefs have too quickly transformed into actions. The ignoramuses and truth-deniers have been labelled as 'infidels' or 'heretics' and passages have been found in holy books to condone and encourage persecution, hatred and even violence towards the other group.

I used the past tense to take the sting out of these last few sentences, but we only have to switch on the news to see that it still happens today – in every corner of the world.

Of course, persecution and discrimination are not the sole domain of the world of religion. It occurs in any situation where one group genuinely believes that they are fundamentally superior to another.

On 26 January 1788, Australia was 'founded'. It had been 'discovered' 18 years previously. The 'discovery' and the subsequent 'founding' were both news to the estimated 750,000 people whose ancestors had been inhabiting the continent for tens of thousands of years before the self-titled 'First Fleet' arrived in Botany Bay. The new white settlers believed in their innate superiority so unequivocally that they labelled the new continent 'terra nullius' (no man's land). The aborigines were not only regarded as being inferior to the white man, they weren't even human. Numerous tribes across the country were exterminated, especially if they retaliated. The sustainability and power of a hardened belief are not to be underestimated: Australia's aborigines were not included in the official Australian census until 1967.

The Federation of Australia was formed on 1 January 1901 with a brand new constitution. It included a section (Section 25) that explicitly penalized States if they were to exclude anyone from voting on account of their race. That's a good thing, obviously, but it also shows that at the time excluding people on account of their race was common practice. The reason for the clause was to discourage the practice of racial exclusion; however, it didn't outlaw it. Another section (Section 51 Clause 26) was explicitly racist, authorizing legislation with respect to 'people of any race for whom it is deemed necessary to make special laws'. Sir Edmund Barton, Australia's first prime minister, told the 1897–98 constitutional convention that Section 51 was needed so that the Commonwealth could 'regulate the affairs of the people of coloured or inferior races who are in the Commonwealth'. Both sections still exist today.

One of the first pieces of legislation declared by the first Australian Federal Government back in 1901 was the Immigration Restriction Act, which allowed for the restriction of immigration on the basis of race. (Something Prime Minister Modi of India only recently adopted with neigh-bouring Muslims in his sights.) Subsequent acts further strengthened the policy, giving British migrants preference over all others.

Eighteen years after Australian Federation, at the 1919 Paris Peace Conference following the First World War, Japan recommended that a declaration be added to the Treaty of Versailles. 'The Racial Equality Proposal' was a proposal designed to abolish racial discrimination among all members of the League of Nations. The Prime Minister of Australia and the President of the United States both vetoed the proposal.

Just let that sink in for a second.

Thankfully, the principle of racial equality would be revisited after the Second World War and incorporated into the United Nations Charter in 1945 as the fundamental principle of international justice.

Even though during the Second World War, Australia's Prime Minister, John Curtin, declared that Australia 'shall remain forever the home of the descendants of those people who came here in peace in order to establish in the South Seas an outpost of the British race', I am pleased to say that succes-sive governments subsequently dismantled this 'White Australia Policy' between 1949 and 1966. Finally, in 1975, 187 years after British occupation and 74 years after Federation, the Whitlam Government passed the Racial Discrimination Act, which made racially based selection criteria unlawful.

A hardened belief can take some time to dismantle!

A hardened belief can take some time to dismantle!

In the decades since, Australia has maintained large-scale multi-ethnic immigration, allowing people from any country to apply to migrate to Australia, regardless of their nationality, ethnicity, culture, religion or language. Some 28 per cent of Australia's resident population was born overseas. Net migration into Australia was 237,000 in 2018. At 45 immigrants per 1,000 inhabitants, its net immigration is one of the highest in the Western world; three times that of the United States and the UK.

Imagine...

Let's imagine a different world, one in which we all adhered to two simple, mutually enriching philosophies:

1 Non-violence: towards ourselves and to others.
2 Truthfulness: again, to ourselves and to others but with an additional caveat that we recognize that your truth may be different from my truth – and that's OK – as long as our different versions of the truth don't hurt anyone.[3]

Imagine such a world. A world where nations didn't automatically consider themselves to be superior or exceptional. A world without 'White Supremacism'. A world without terrorism – Islamic, loyalist, republican or any other variety. A world where the terms 'blasphemer' and 'infidel' were embarrassing words from a bygone era. A world where race is simply not an issue. A world without soaring and dangerously manipulative nationalistic rhetoric. Imagine if our political leaders followed a doctrine of non-violence, authenticity and an appreciation that someone else's truth may be just as valid as theirs. Trade wars would be a thing of the past. Arms manufacturers would be a tiny part of our economies.

Imagine…

Overcoming your negative thoughts

Change your thoughts and you change your world. NORMAN VINCENT PEALE[4]

Our thoughts can transmogrify into beliefs, beliefs can become 'truth' and 'truth' can lead to action. The resulting actions of our beliefs can be socially constructive – to adopt a child or raise money for charity – or they can be socially destructive – to strap explosives to our chest and walk into a crowded marketplace.

We have the power to change our thoughts and once we recognize this, we can change our world – for the better.

The first step is to detach yourself from your negative thoughts to see them as they really are – simply stories.

We can change our thoughts. We can challenge our beliefs – without losing face or our sense of personal integrity. We can start to listen to other viewpoints – not just to reply, but to understand.

In order to change our behaviours, in order to change unwanted actions or results, we also need to look at the thoughts, feelings and beliefs that have led us to behave in this manner.

I am not for one minute positing that all thoughts and beliefs are bad or wrong. But they need to be the start of a conversation, not the end of one. This requires the opinion-holder to countenance the idea that their belief is not immutable; that it could be amended if a new set of facts and circumstances arose. When someone says, 'Well, that's my opinion', they are generally shutting down any discussion on the matter in question. They are setting up a no-win, adversarial conflict or retreating into their bunker and preparing to come through any attack unscathed.

Opinions and beliefs are just thoughts that have been strengthened in our minds.

Opinions and beliefs are just thoughts that have been strengthened in our minds. We need to be open to the possibility that they may be wrong.

Good scientists do this naturally. The scientific method is to propose a hypothesis, a theory, and then look for empirical evidence to prove or disprove this theory. Good scientists are 'wrong' all the time. They like being wrong because that is how they learn. That is how they progress. That is how they succeed. Good scientists succeed in one 'failure' after another.

The stories that we tell ourselves are not 'the truth'. Neither are our opinions. For example, if we continually tell ourselves that we will be blamed for the way things currently work if we were to relent to change, this will eventually become a belief, a 'hardened fact' in our minds and it will cause us to push back on new ideas and even attack those who are proposing them.

The same is true when it comes to any major social, political or religious issue. Simply entertaining the idea that our opinions and beliefs to do with climate change, foreigners, Islam, Christianity, Judaism... may not be entirely accurate would be an incredibly enlightening step. Our world would suddenly be a very different place.

If we start to see our thoughts and our beliefs as yet-to-be-verified theories rather than universal truths that are intertwined with our identity; if we regard our thoughts and our beliefs as incomplete stories; we can begin to be open to all sorts of new possibilities.

We can open the door to positive change.

The power of self-belief

Ironically, a key enabler of our ability to overcome the barriers we erect to change is a belief: a belief in yourself. Because we only change if we want to. And you will only want to once you believe you should – and can.

Self-belief is a force that creates wonders. Apple, the world's first US $1 trillion business, was the result of two men who believed that they could change the world – Steve Jobs and Steve Wozniak. The world's second US $1 trillion business, Microsoft, was also the result in Bill Gates' belief in himself. Ditto with Amazon and Jeff Bezos. JK Rowling believed in herself so much that she invented new worlds and new characters that captivated the planet, selling 500 million books, umpteen billion Lego bricks and creating one of history's most successful movie franchises in the process.

To overcome any barrier to change, especially when it is big change, we need to dig deep and find the core part of us that is unique and strong – and we all have it. We then need to like and value what we find so that we can build upon it. We need to believe that we can overcome the barriers in front of us. We need to trust in our 'true self', trust in our ability to cope with change, trust in our ability to embrace the change and look for opportunities, trust in our ability to 'succeed', however we choose to define 'success'.

To overcome any barrier to change, especially when it is big change, we need to dig deep and find the core part of us that is unique and strong.

But this confidence needs to be 'eyes wide open' confidence – a confidence based on an understanding of our own limitations and an appreciation of the challenges ahead of us. Blind confidence is empty. 'Eyes-wide-open' confidence is sustainable as it is based on an assessment of strengths and challenges – and hard work.

And 'eyes-wide-open' confidence is entirely justified, for it lies within every one of us. Every single one of us has the ability to be our own catalyst for change.

Pausing for reflection

We have covered a lot of ground in this part so far. So let's pause and review some of the salient points.

Each of us erects barriers to change. The barriers will vary depending upon the change in question and each of us will favour one or two default barriers – our 'go to' change barriers, if you like.

The first step to overcoming any change barrier is to shine a light on it and acknowledge its existence. But we must do this in a way that is non-judgemental. It's not our fault that we erect barriers to change. It is the way we are wired. It is entirely normal. Sometimes it is even healthy. After all, not every change is 'good'. But even when a change is 'bad', we must react to it – and how we react can make all the difference. We will need to overcome our barriers to change.

The pithy summary of how to do that is below:

- Admit denial.
- Observe our emotions – STOP.

- Confront our fears:
  - fear of failure: put things into perspective; bite-size chunks;
  - fear of blame: become part of the solution;
  - fear of the unknown: make the unknown familiar.
- Find good tribes.
- Reframe our identity.
- Test our doubts.
- Detach from our negative thoughts – see them as the stories they are.

Figure 21.1 is a template setting out a change strategy that you can download and use.

FIGURE 21.1 Template for change strategy

Overcoming the barriers we erect to change

change | strategy
www.changeandstrategy.com

Barriers to change	Reflections and score out of 10	Tactics for overcoming the barrier	Actions
Denial		Admit denial	
Emotions		Observe your emotions	
Fear of failure		Put things into perspective	
Fear of blame		Be part of the solution	
Fear of the unknown		Make the unknown familiar	
Fear of others		Find good tribes	
Identity		Find the help you need	
Doubts		Test them before accepting them	
Negative thoughts		See them as the stories they are	

Download this template from www.changeandstrategy.com

CHAPTER TWENTY-TWO

The power of yoga

Change is not something that we should fear.
Rather, it is something that we should welcome. For without
change, nothing in this world would ever grow or blossom,
and no one in this world would ever move forward to become
the person they're meant to be. BKS IYENGAR[1]

I f you wish to improve your ability to cope with and embrace change, it is pretty hard to find a better solution than yoga.

Yoga helps to release tension in your mind and body. It helps us to put things into perspective and calm our mind – for it is only when our mind is calm that we can work out how we are going to react to the change. And, as we have discussed many times through-out the book, how we react to change is the secret ingredient that can make all the difference.

I have engaged the assistance of an expert to help me with this chapter – my wife, Jane – who has been a qualified yoga teacher since 2005 and a qualified yoga therapist since 2012. She holds yoga classes and yoga therapy sessions from her yoga studio in Oxfordshire and runs yoga retreats several times a year in various locations around the world including Kerala, Marrakesh, Mallorca, Bali and Cornwall. She is also an examiner at London's Yoga Campus.

How we react to change is the secret ingredient that can make all the difference.

Jane helps her clients become physically and mentally stronger. She helps people to help themselves to recover from, or manage, any number of big, dramatic, 'Burning Platform' changes – anxiety, depression, death of a loved one, cancer, physical injuries…

The following few pages are the summary of my interview with Jane about the power of yoga to help us embrace even the most challenging changes in our lives.

Yoga's principles

Yoga is based on two core principles:

1 Abhyasa: the need to practise and become adept at achieving a state of complete tranquility, of being in a stable place.
2 Vairagya: non-attachment, the letting go of aversions, fears, false identities, the need for material things, as these provide a veil over our true self.

The actual purpose of the physical postures, the yoga poses, the asanas, is to help us to become strong and free from physical distractions, so we can calm our breathing and reach a state of tranquillity.

Then we can start to detach, to realize that our thoughts are just thoughts – and that they don't define us. We can just observe them without getting emotionally attached to them.

It helps us free ourselves from identifying with 'attachments' – both physical and mental. It frees us from our in-built 'conditioning'. We are all conditioned through our memories, our upbringing, our education, our experiences. Yoga can help us identify our true self within a still, quiet, tranquil place. It can help us discover the true essence of who we really are.

I often start an evening class with a simple practice to help people calm the 'chattering of their minds' as Patanjali[2] put it. My students have been busy all day and their minds are still busy – thinking about their day or the row they had with their partner or the mayhem of their kids' dinner time – their brains are buzzing. So I say, 'You might be here physically but you're not here mentally. Your mind is not here. It is either in the past or the future. And yoga is about being in the present moment'.

During the first few minutes of a class, I invite everyone to 'arrive on their mat'. I ask them to lie down, focus on their breathing and connect with how their body feels. Enabling the mind to focus on the physical brings the mind into the present and helps the body to calm. An amazing transformation occurs in just a few short minutes; their breathing slows, their bodies unwind and I can almost feel the buzzing in their minds start to fade.

If our mind is agitated, our breathing tends to be rapid and shallow and our body starts to tense up. It is impossible to calm the mind if your body is feeling tight, tense or uncomfortable; if your breathing is shallow or fast. To calm the body we must calm the mind – and vice versa. The mind and the body are two sides of the same coin.

When we worry, we tend to ruminate; our thoughts going around and around in our heads incessantly. Sometimes we can't switch our brains off at night and we find it difficult to sleep, which of course only makes matter worse. It can even get to the point where these ruminating thoughts induce anxiety or panic attacks. Sometimes we reach for alcohol or sleeping pills to try to stop the incessant rumination. But that is only a temporary fix. Sometimes we reach for material things; we buy a sports car or a boat in the vain hope that these things will make a difference. But they don't. Often, they are just big, expensive band-aids.

Separating you from your thoughts

Our thoughts aren't us. They are impermanent. Yet too often we let them define us. The solution is to be able to see these thoughts for what they are and to do what we can to calm the body, calm the mind and detach ourselves from them; acknowledge their presence and observe them – without judgement. In this simple act of obser-vation, we realize that our thoughts are not us. They are separate entities entirely.

A negative thought is not your thought. It is just a thought.

Thoughts creep into our minds all the time. Don't fight them. Let them in. By all means, welcome them in the front door but open the back door so they can leave as quickly as they came. If you don't give your negative thoughts your atten-tion, your energy – they will fade. They may even leave completely.

I learnt a simple yet powerful technique from an excellent Michael Stone mindfulness course.[3] Instead of giving our thoughts labels such as 'anger' or 'fear', his suggestion was to simply label them 'thinking thinking' or 'reac-tion reaction'. Doing this will take the sting out of them; take the emotion out of them; stop them from being personal.

A negative thought is not *your* thought. It is just *a* thought.

Separating the person from the pain, ailment or disease

The concept of detachment is fundamental to yoga therapy. If someone is very ill and has been in pain for a long time, they tend to identify with the pain; they tend to identify with the ailment. The pain or the disease starts to become part of their identity: 'I am someone with chronic back pain. I am someone with cancer.' What I help my yoga therapy clients to do is to turn those thoughts around.

I love the way Hippocrates[4] phrased it almost 2,500 years ago: 'It is more important to know what person has the disease than what disease the person has.'

As a yoga therapist, my job is to try to separate my client from their ailment; separate themselves from their pain.

Often, clients have been exhausting themselves thinking over and over again about their ailment. So, I first help them to practise poses that might help their bodies feel better – focusing on what they *can* do not what they *can't* do.

Once they start to feel better physically, they can then focus on their breathing. The breathing of someone who is caught up in pain tends to be shallow and quick. Anxious breathing expends so much energy without getting a great deal of energy into our body in return.

When we sit quietly and breathe deeply and slowly, we are able to find that lovely still point. So I help my clients to focus on exhalation (people tend to forget about the exhalation breath); to breathe using their diaphragm; to breathe in through their nose and out through a little hole in their lips, visualizing that there is a little golden thread extending from their mouth – all techniques to refocus the mind away from the pain and be in the present moment.

The aim of mindfulness techniques such as these is to help someone in chronic pain to live with the pain; to live with the disease. I can't get rid of pain. I'm not a painkiller, I'm a yoga therapist. I ask them to: 'Look at the pain. Sit with it. Watch it. Walk around it like you're walking around a beautiful piece of sculpture. Look at it from above. Look at it from below. Look at it from the sides. Then start to observe it as it is. Don't give it the status it craves.'

Doing this, we can start to look at it objectively and begin to think, 'Yes this is pain but actually, it's all right'.

People not only feel different after a yoga therapy session, they can look physically different as well – they look calmer, the colour has come back into their cheeks, they are smiling. They are often a very different person from the one who walked through the door. But they need to keep practising, which is why as yoga therapists we provide our clients with a written practice to use at home. Regular practice can help them achieve a permanent shift in their state of mind and body.

Parinama: recognizing things are always changing

Yoga teaches us to use our energy, our intelligence and our awareness to recognize that things are always changing and then make choices that help us either cope with or make that change.

It helps us to say: 'OK, this change is happening to me. I might not like it but let's just come back to the fact that change is inevitable. It's how I react to the change that is important.'

Yoga helps us to view our thoughts and emotions objectively and see the bigger picture.

If I am caught up in anger, fear, resentment or negative thoughts then I am not going to react very well to change. I'm probably going to push it away, perhaps even saying and doing things that I shouldn't. When it comes to big change that has been forced upon us, negativity can take control.

Yoga helps people take a little step back; to take a couple of deep breaths, pause, and then take another look at the situation. Maybe it isn't all bad. Maybe some good will even come from the change.

Yoga helps us to view our thoughts and emotions objectively and see the bigger picture. It helps us to approach the change as an independent observer, not as someone who is a victim of it.

It helps us to welcome the change.

Jane Macpherson
www.janemacphersonyoga.co.uk

PART FIVE

Be your own Change Catalyst

No one saves us but ourselves.
No one can and no one may. We ourselves must walk the path. BUDDHA

OK. We have explored our personal barriers to change and we have
discussed ways to overcome each one of them.

It is now time for action. And you are in the driver's seat. You will have to be
your own change leader. No-one is more motivated or better suited to the role.

So with that in mind, I would now like to share some additional skills,
tools and ideas that you may find valuable in your quest to embrace change:

1 resilience;
2 creating favourable conditions for change (featuring HENRY);
3 finding the help you need;
4 helping others;
5 your personal SWOT and strategic plan;
6 treat yourself like a change project.

Let's explore each one.

CHAPTER TWENTY-THREE

Resilience

Do not judge me by my success.
Judge me by how many times I fell down and got
back up again. NELSON MANDELA[1]

Resilience, ably supported by its synergistic side-kick, 'self-confidence', is the most important ingredient of successful and sustainable personal change. It is the ubiquitous watermark, the often unspoken word that permeates every chapter of this book.

Resilience is our ability to get back up again when fate deals us a nasty blow. It is our ability to cope with life's ups and downs. It is our ability to cope with and embrace change.

The year 2019 marked the 75th anniversary of the D-Day landings in Normandy; the daring campaign that was the moment that the European theatre of the Second World War started to turn in the allies' favour. In commemorating this pivotal moment of that pivotal war, much was made of the heroism of the veterans; those still with us were centre-stage at the official celebrations. They were described in almost every paper and on every news bulletin as 'the resilient generation'.

The D-Day veterans were brave, full of purpose – and yes, resilient. In fact, this term could be applied to the entire British population at the time. The British were resilient in the face of air raids, food shortages, disease, poverty, innumerable deaths, unbelievable violence, devastating destruction and the potential annihilation of their democracy, their nation and their way of life. Obviously, resilience wasn't and isn't solely a British trait; the same adjective could be used for swathes of people across the whole of Europe during this horrible period in our history; a period that I sincerely hope we will never repeat. 'Hope' is the most positive word I can find to use here as Brexit (and President Trump) have made me far less confident in our ability to maintain international peace. One of the striking sights from the D-Day celebrations were the tears of veterans exasperated at the UK's decision to leave the EU. Those who have actually put their lives on the line for British democracy and peace across Europe have seen what happens when we take peace for granted. They do not want to erect any barriers to collaboration with their neighbours. Meanwhile, those fervently in favour of Brexit use the Second World War rhetoric to incite 'the Blitz spirit' and portray Brexit as 'Britain vs the EU'. Boris Johnson, once Brexit Minister and now Prime Minister for perhaps the next decade, has even compared the EU to Nazi Germany, accused it of 'bullying' Britain and described a bill to request an extension of EU membership to ward off a so-called 'No Deal' departure from the union as 'the surrender bill'. The key difference is, of course, that the D-Day veterans were fighting *for* Europe, not against it. In the face of constant change, of a magnitude and ferocity that my generation and those younger than me find almost impossible to imagine, they were resilient. They kept calm and they carried on.

As I watched the D-Day commemorations, this word, resilience, struck a chord. To cope with change, we must all have resilience. Change is inevitable. 'Bad' change will happen to us. 'Good' change will also happen to us. We will instigate change ourselves – and not all of these changes will work out as we had anticipated. Consequently, one of the most important skills of all is… resilience.

To cope with change, we must all have resilience. Change is inevitable.

It made me wonder whether the generations that followed the Second World War have become progressively less resilient. As we have become progressively wealthier; as food rationing has morphed into abundance; as killer diseases are being eradicated; as antibiotics have stopped previously fatal infections in their tracks; as lifespans have increased dramatically; as our standards of living have improved from one generation to the next… has each generation also become less resilient than its predecessor?

My grandparents' generation, the generation that endured the Second World War, were born more than a century ago into an age before antibiotics and widespread vaccinations; an age when the average life expectancy of a newborn was not much more than 40. Infections could be fatal, as could childbirth for mother and child. If you survived your first five years, infections, disease, malnutrition and war were waiting in the wings. They 'made do', went without, set 'low' expectations (if you can call fighting for world peace a low expectation…) and rarely complained.

My parents' generation came to adulthood in the 1950s and 1960s and created a brave new world of exploding prosperity. They put a man on the moon and, if they were too old to be drafted to fight an unconscionable war in Vietnam (for Australian and US readers), enjoyed an astonishing period of relative global peace. Mind you, they did come awfully close to nuclear war at one point!

My generation came to adulthood in the ambitious 1980s, discovered credit cards, embraced debt, property ownership, international travel, leveraged investment, computers, fax machines, DVDs, CD-ROMs, email, mobile phones and the internet. To the vast majority of us, war is an unimaginable horror that is both intangible and surreal.

Our children have grown up in a world that their great-grandparents could hardly have imagined; a world of abundance, of unprecedented power at their fingertips, of global interconnectivity, of science that looks more like magic every day, of bewildering choices, of almost limitless potential in comparison to the war era.

Each generation – as relative peace, prosperity and longevity have all advanced – has dared to dream bigger dreams. Compared to the D-Day veterans, perhaps it is inevitable that we have become a little 'softer'. But maybe this is the wrong way to look at it. The challenges of many of today's generation may not be immediate 'life or death'; their challenges are on higher levels of the Maslow hierarchy.[2] Meeting today's challenges requires a different type of resilience. Perhaps the qualities of stoicism and preternatural patience that the Second World War veterans needed in 1940 aren't the best tools for success in 2020. Perhaps the Millennials are just as resilient as their forebears – but the nature of the resilience has changed.

The Millennials: snowflakes or saviours?

Many of today's social commentators look at the latest generation to reach adulthood and see an 'entitled, self-centred, unfocused and lazy'[3] generation; one that is far too quick to diagnose mental illness, far too precious and 'politically correct',[4] unwilling to start at the bottom, unwilling to 'do the hard yards' and unwilling to stick at a job they don't like. They see a generation of 'snowflakes'; a generation that is unaccustomed to failure and too brittle to cope with setbacks. They see a generation that has lost the art of resilience.

Before I explain why I profoundly disagree with this damning and spurious assessment of a generation that I not only admire but believe will actually save this planet of ours; before I dismiss this popular critique of Millennials as too simplistic and simply too easy – let's take a look at the main arguments against this generation. Of course, every credible story is based on some element of truth; every superficial analysis is based to some degree on facts that are inevitably misrepresented in the process...

The 'Millennials are Snowflakes' argument goes something like this...

The Millennials have been subject to several 'failed parenting strategies'.[5] My generation is accused of bringing up our kids to believe that they can do anything; anything is possible. In other words, we are accused of setting unrealistic expectations, thereby almost certainly dooming them to disappointment and failure. To make matters worse, we are also accused of never letting our kids experience failure (participation medals, ribbons for coming fourth...) so that when they don't live up to their unrealistic expectations, they crash big time.

This latest generation has been brought up to believe that if they work hard, get good grades and obtain a good degree, the world is their oyster.[6] Therefore, the argument goes, when our little darlings finally arrive at the workplace, they experience an almighty shock when they discover that they have to start at the bottom, that 'they're not special, their mums can't get them a promotion, that you get nothing for coming in last and by the way you can't just have it because you want it'.[7]

It is certainly true that the latest generation has grown up in a world of instant gratification and 24/7 connectivity – neither of which on its own is particularly healthy but together they are a toxic combination. Being always on and always distracted hampers calmness, downtime and innovation.

It is also true that reliance on, and addiction to, mobile phones are serious issues, and this generation is the first to experience it. In his interview with 'Inside Quest', Simon Sinek talks about a 2012 Harvard study that reported that 'talking about oneself through social media activates a pleasure sensation in the brain (via a hit of dopamine) usually associated with food, money and sex'. Dopamine is highly addictive. He also claims that even though kids know that their 'friend-ships' online are superficial, 'the trauma for kids to be unfriended can be too much to handle'.

Being always on and always distracted hampers calmness, downtime and innovation.

Simon portrays a picture of a generation that is fragile, lacking in confidence, never content and devoid of resilience; a generation that has been 'dealt a bad hand' and needs help. He implores business leaders to 'help this amazing, idealistic, fantastic generation build their confidence, learn patience, learn the social skills, find a better balance between life and technology'.

When I first watched his interview, I applauded his insight and analysis. Upon reflection, I have a number of issues with it – and I have come to a very different conclusion.

The Millennials are no more 'entitled' than the graduates of 20 years ago. When I was a Senior Manager at Andersen Consulting back in the late 1990s, every new batch of highly intelligent and ambitious consultants came into the firm with expectations sky high. They didn't want to be preparing the slides for presentations. They wanted to be presenting to the CEO. They, too, didn't want to put in the hard yards. But they swiftly discovered that, if they wished to be successful, there was no other way.

What I dislike about the analysis is that it paints Millennials as victims, which is both untrue and unhelpful. They're not victims at all. They have been dealt the alleged 'bad hand' of peace, safety, world travel, love, affec-tion,[8] relative abundance and incredible technological wizardry – incredible gifts that obviously come with their own set of consequences and challenges. Yes, their challenges are different from ours, but they recognize these chal-lenges and they are working to overcome them – just like we did and just like our parents did. They are simply doing it in a different way, which makes complete sense seeing as they are tackling very different challenges.

Yes, this latest generation's challenges have the potential to affect their confidence and their ability to form meaningful relationships. Yes, they need to understand the difference and find a better balance between real life and technology. But they are not only learning this, they are acting upon it. Yes, they are impatient and idealistic – two of the things I love about them the most.

And of course business leaders should help their young workers to build confidence, patience, develop social skills and improve balance. They should help every worker to do this!

It is true that many leaders find their Millennial employees to be especially challenging, not only because they have a completely different set of values but also because values are very important to this next generation – much more important than they were to the generation who joined the workforce during the 'Greed is Good!'[9] 1980s.

As I mentioned in Part One, when my generation joined the workforce, we simply wanted to make a living. This generation wants to make a difference. If their employer's values don't match theirs, or if they feel the company's leaders aren't living up to the stated corporate values, or if the purpose of the company isn't greater than profit or shareholder value, they will leave.

Unlike mine, this latest generation has come into the world of work with a burning desire for work–life balance from the get-go. Some of my generation despair at this, and yet they know full well that it is the right approach – as we have been striving, and failing, to achieve it for decades.

Yes, as a rash generalization (as any discussion of 'generations' inevitably is), Millennials are impatient; they get bored easily. Good on them. I don't see this as a negative. I see this as ambitious. This generation will not only have several jobs in their lifetime; they will have several completely different careers. They work out what they want and then, rather than sticking at a job that isn't heading in the right direction, they find a job that is.

When it comes to 'employer loyalty', they are far savvier than we were at their age. They have entered the workforce with the full understanding that the golden era of employee and employer loyalty is over. They have started the first of their many careers with their eyes wide open. They have seen their parents' generation laid off at a moment's notice and without adequate assistance. They have seen countless business magnates abuse inadequate corporate laws to rob their previously loyal employees of their pension monies, their jobs and/or their hope. Sometimes all three.

This generation will not rely on the 'loyalty' of their employers. They know their future is up to them. They will have numerous employers. They will switch from full-time to part-time and back again. They will become contractors. They will take career breaks. This requires a form of resilience that is foreign to previous generations. My grandparents' generation put up with an incredible amount of hardship. They were loyal – to their nation and to their employers. Their resilience was stoic. The Millennials have an international mind-set and won't put up with a load of disingenuous nonsense from their employers.

The golden era of employee and employer loyalty is over.

Their form of resilience is based on something that one could argue is even more valuable – it is based on self-belief.

Strategies for enhancing your resilience

If we want to improve our ability to cope with and embrace change, we need to build our resilience – regardless of our age, background or situation. The American Psychological Association (APA) concludes that key factors associated with resilience are:

- The capacity to make realistic plans and take steps to carry them out.
- A positive view of yourself and confidence in your strengths and abilities.
- Skills in communication and problem solving.
- The capacity to manage strong feelings and impulses.

They also state that 'all of these are factors that people can develop in themselves'.[10]

Obviously, we are all different; an approach to building resilience that works for one person may not work for another.

But here is a baker's dozen of tips, courtesy of the APA and the Mayo Clinic:[11]

1 **Remain hopeful.** You can't change the past, but you can look towards the future. Accepting and even anticipating change makes it easier to adapt and view new challenges with less anxiety.

2 **Make connections.** Relationships are important. Learn to accept help and support from others will strengthen your resilience.

3 **Choose how you react.** Even the largest of crises are not insurmountable problems. The APA declares: 'You can't change the fact that highly stressful events happen, but you can change how you interpret and respond to these events'.

4 **Accept that change is a part of life.** Certain goals may no longer be attainable as a result of adverse situations. Accepting circumstances that cannot be changed can help you focus on circumstances that you can alter.

5 **Keep things in perspective.** Even when facing very painful events, try to consider the stressful situation in a broader context and keep a long-term perspective. Avoid blowing the event out of proportion.

6 **Forward momentum in small steps.** Move towards your goals. Develop some realistic goals. Do something regularly – even if it seems like a small accomplishment – that enables you to move towards your goals. Instead of focusing on tasks that seem unachievable, ask yourself, 'What's one thing I know I can accomplish today that helps me move in the direction I want to go?'

7 **Take decisive actions.** Act on adverse situations as much as you can. Take decisive actions, rather than burying your head in the sand and hoping problems will just go away.

8 **Make every day meaningful.** Do something that gives you a sense of accomplishment and purpose every day. Set goals to help you look towards the future with meaning.

9 **Learn from experience.** Think of how you've coped with hardships in the past. Consider the skills and strategies that helped you through rough times. You might even write about past experiences in a journal to help you identify positive and negative behaviour patterns – and guide your future behaviour.

10 **Look for opportunities for self-discovery.** People often learn something about themselves and may find that they have grown in some respect as a result of their struggle with difficult change. Many people who have experienced tragedies and hardship have reported better relationships, greater sense of strength even while feeling vulnerable, increased sense of self-worth, a more developed spirituality and heightened appreciation for life.

11 **Nurture a positive view of yourself.** Developing confidence in your ability to solve problems and trusting your instincts helps build resilience.

12 **Take care of yourself.** Pay attention to your own needs and feelings. Engage in activities that you enjoy and find relaxing. Exercise regularly. Taking care of yourself helps to keep your mind and body primed to deal with situations that require resilience.

13 **Be proactive.** Don't ignore your problems. Instead, figure out what needs to be done, make a plan and take action. Although it can take time to recover from a major setback, traumatic event or loss, know that your situation can improve if you work at it.

CHAPTER TWENTY-FOUR

Creating favourable conditions for change

*The core job of a change leader is to help people to want to change,
and then help them to work out how.
You can be your own change leader.* CAMPBELL MACPHERSON

HENRY

'Healthy Start, Brighter Future.'

I would like to introduce you to HENRY, a remarkable UK charity with a mission 'to support families to provide a healthy, happy start for their children and lay the foundations for a brighter future'.[1]

They provide timely support to vulnerable families in deprived communities, helping to build their skills, knowledge and confidence to give their children a healthy start, helping them flourish throughout childhood and beyond. This helps protects children from obesity, tooth extraction, poor mental wellbeing, and more.

The aspect of their work I want to talk about in this chapter is their efforts in tackling childhood obesity. They help parents to change. They help them to want to change. And they help them to act. They give them the why and the how but perhaps more important than everything else – they help parents to remove obstacles and create the right environment for change to be able to happen.

FIGURE 24.1 The HENRY approach

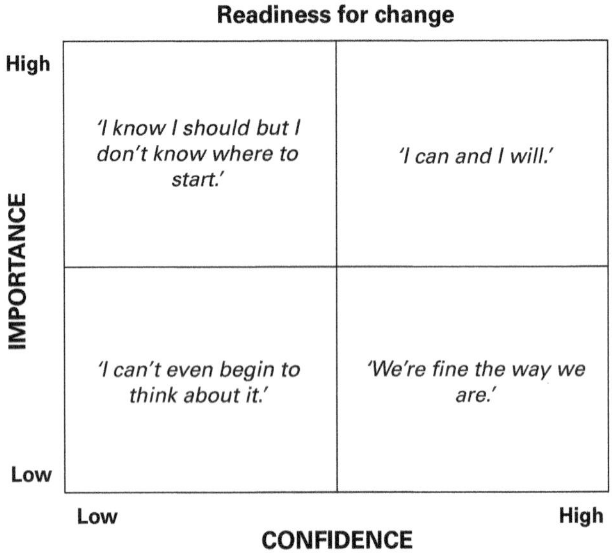

Readiness for change

	Low → CONFIDENCE → High	
High IMPORTANCE	'I know I should but I don't know where to start.'	'I can and I will.'
Low	'I can't even begin to think about it.'	'We're fine the way we are.'

Their approach starts with the premise that resistance to change is 'natural rather than pathological', which removes blame from the discussion entirely. They note that all of us at one time or another have procrastinated, made excuses, justified inaction or simply buried our heads in the sand, even when we can see that breaking old habits would have been in our best interests.

It's back to the joke about social workers and light bulbs – we have to want to change.

HENRY uses a neat 2 × 2 to illustrate readiness for change (Figure 24.1).

This simple diagram shows that if it isn't genuinely important to someone, they simply won't change. As one HENRY health visitor describes such an interaction, 'I sit there and give her advice and I know she's not going to follow any of it'.

Not only do we need to understand why changing is important and how to change, we also need the desire to change.

There is a hidden secret behind both of the axes in the above matrix that HENRY practitioners fully understand – facts alone will not increase the levels of importance or confidence. Not only do we need to understand why changing is important and how to change, we also need the desire to change.

HENRY's practitioners work on all of these levels. They impart the knowledge of why the change should occur, the facts of what to do and the understanding of how to bring about the change, plus they also work with parents to help them build the genuine desire for change.

How and when they do this is often more important than the information they impart:

> If a parent is struggling to cope, rushing in with lots of advice, however well-intentioned, is likely to increase feelings of emotional overload, shame or guilt. Our desire to help can inadvertently push parents away: urging them to make changes to their family lifestyle may well be perceived as a criticism of the way they are bringing up their children and is likely to be met with defensiveness.[2]

HENRY's people are taught to look for and address the underlying resistance to change. 'For example, if a parent is too overwhelmed to change, we can focus on helping them to reduce stress. If they lack confidence, helping them to recognize their strengths will build self-confidence.' Sometimes hitting the problem head-on just won't work.

It's not as simple as telling the parents to cook more, cut out sweets, give their kids a balanced diet and help them get more exercise. While this is entirely logical, as we have discussed many times – we humans don't work that way.

HENRY practitioners explore a wide range of related issues that affect a child's weight and health. They explore the social and cultural context, the family's default habits and attitudes, parenting skills, medical issues, nutrition, activity levels and behaviours as well as physical and emotional development of the children. In other words, they really do their homework on every key factor that may be influencing the child's eating habits. There is no point trying to come up with a solution until you have completely diagnosed the problem. So HENRY practitioners help parents to look at all of the factors that may be contributing to their children's obesity – and then work out what and how to change.

They review the social and cultural context (accessibility of fresh food close to home, religious and cultural customs affecting how the family eats, opportunities for outdoor activities and play, financial concerns and employment shift patterns). They look at whether the family sits down and eats together, how they spend their leisure time, how food is used, and the attitudes to food on the family. They observe their confidence as a parent, the approach to rules and the influence of other family members. They look at mental health and learning difficulties. They look at eating skills, behaviour at mealtimes, conflict resolution and sleep habits. And armed with this detailed insight, HENRY's professionals then help the parents create the right conditions for change to occur.

People don't change because they are told to. They change because, and when, they want to. To help turn this desire into action, we need a supportive environment and the space and opportunity to think through how we can remove the obstacles to change and how we can create new habits. Note it isn't the HENRY practitioner who is providing all of the answers; it is the parent. Do they think reducing screen time would help? Eating as a family? Engaging the kids in the cooking? Replacing sweets with carrot sticks? Eating earlier? …

Sometimes the best solutions are the least expected. One mother made an enormous difference to her children simply by changing the route she walked home from school every evening – one that did not pass by KFC.

Which obstacles to change could you remove for yourself? Which rituals and routines are currently getting in the way of you embracing the change you know you need? What could you do to create a better environment that would help, not hinder, the change?

What's your equivalent of 'no longer walking past KFC'?

CHAPTER TWENTY-FIVE

Finding the help you need

*I asked for help, which is the hardest thing
in the world.* MARCIA WALLACE[1]

We can see from the last chapter just how important it is to find the help we need to change. Yes, we need to take responsibility for changing, but part of that responsibility includes finding someone to help us.

If we need help and it is nowhere to be found, we can often give up at the first hurdle. Our internal resistance to change is that strong.

All meaningful change involves a loss of something. Even when the gains outweigh the losses, the gain is a *net* gain; eg if you receive a promotion at work, your pay will most likely increase as will your responsibilities and status, but you are also likely to be stepping out of your comfort zone. The fear of having reached your 'Peter Plateau' may be overwhelming.[2] Every change has its downsides, even good change. Good change involves taking a risk and even a net gain includes a loss of some sort.

All meaningful change involves a loss of something.

If we genuinely want to change, we will need to face the change demons we discussed in Parts Three and Four: our fears, our emotions, our doubts, our negative thoughts, how we see our identity, the trough.

And it is so much easier if we have someone to help us navigate the change.

'Be strong enough to stand alone, smart enough to know when you need help and brave enough to ask for it.'[3]

No-one is an island. We all need help at times. There is nothing wrong with that. It's healthy. If the person or entity that is bringing this change down upon you has neglected to provide you with any assistance to cope with it, then it is up to you to find some. Find a coach, talk to friends, find a yoga therapist, read and re-read this book and others like it – work out what help you need and go and get it.

Even if you are the one instigating the change on yourself, you will still find that assistance is invaluable – talk to friends, engage a coach to assist you. Several brains are always better than one.

Reaching out to people in times of stress or change is actually the single most important thing any one of us can do. Let me give you a very graphic example of why this is true.

Suicide is the biggest killer of men under 45 in the UK. Some 5,000 men kill themselves every year. And the single thing that any one of them could have done to save their lives was to open up to someone; to talk; to ask for help. Suicidal thoughts are triggered by big, negative changes that are forced upon people. The three biggest triggers are bereavement, financial/job loss and relationship breakdown. Obviously, only a very small number of us react in this way, but the number who do is increasing. The Ford Clinic in the States has reduced suicide rates among their patients by more than 80 per cent simply by helping them open up to family and friends.

Speaking to other people is that powerful.

CHAPTER TWENTY-SIX

Helping others

*Help others to achieve their dreams and you will
achieve yours.* LES BROWN[1]

Change happens to everyone. Small changes that we must adapt to, small changes that we choose in order to grow and develop, big 'Quantum Leap' change we instigate ourselves and enormous 'Burning Platform' changes that are forced upon us.

Marriage, divorce, birth, death, injury, redundancy, upheaval... every single one of us experiences change.

Helping others to navigate their way through change is not only a wonderful thing to do for a fellow human but it is also highly effective therapy for ourselves – and we usually learn as much, if not more, than the people we are helping. A study reported found that people who described themselves as 'very happy' volunteered at least 5.8 hours a month.[2] The report also found that volunteering can help reduce the symptoms of chronic pain. It can also decrease hypertension.

Even more, it can help us live longer! Regular volunteers show an improved ability to manage stress and stave off disease as well as reduced rates of depression and an increased sense of satisfaction.

Another great thing about altruism is that it is contagious. It causes a chain reaction of other altruistic acts. People are more likely to perform feats of generosity after observing another do the same. This effect can ripple throughout the community, inspiring dozens of individuals to make a difference.[3]

The concept of contagious altruism was the subject of the best-selling book *Pay it Forward* by Catherine Ryan Hyde in 1999.[4]

After the success of the book and the following movie of the same name, Catherine established 'The Pay It Forward Foundation' in September 2000 as 'a catalyst to inspire growth for the Pay It Forward philosophy, acts of kindness among strangers, generating a ripple effect from one person to the next, one community to the next'.[5] Since its inception, the foundation has inspired countless acts of kindness and served to inspire people all over the world to make the 'pay it forward' philosophy part of their lives.

Helping others helps us to focus outwards during change, as the temptation to only see our own issues can be overwhelming.

Helping others also helps enhance our own overall sense of purpose and identity. We are not just a 'parent' or an 'employee'; we are someone who makes a difference.

And as many a teacher will attest, teaching something can be the best way to learn it! Observing someone else's journey through the Change Curve can help us prepare for the same journey. And if you are going through the same change at the same time, two heads and two hearts are so much better than one.

Helping others helps us to focus outwards during change, as the temptation to only see our own issues can be overwhelming. Stepping outside of our own feelings and concerns is healthy – for us and for the person we are helping.

We are all here on earth to help others; what on earth the others are here for I don't know. WH AUDEN[6]

CHAPTER TWENTY-SEVEN

My personal change plan

Knowing yourself is the beginning of all wisdom. ARISTOTLE[1]

We have slayed our fears and we have guided ourselves through the worst of the Change Curve. We have understood what has happened. Now we need to engage the brain and move towards acceptance. We need action. Sometimes, the course of action may be obvious but more often than not, we find we have options – and at this point, they all look equally daunting. As anyone who has tried to buy something from a hypermarket will attest, options can be debilitating.

How on earth do I decide what direction I should head in, let alone the next steps I should take? There are just too many unknowns.

Well maybe we should take a leaf out of the business world for a second and do a little personal 'strategic planning'. A successful strategy always starts with analysis – in this case, a bit of self-reflection; an objective stock-take and analysis of how things currently stand right now. You will need to ask yourself a range of questions and your answers will need to be brutally honest.

In the following example, I have assumed the change in question is employment-related – but of course the headline questions are just as relevant for any significant personal change.

Context

1 **Why is this change happening?** In as detached a manner as possible, seek to understand what happened to bring about this change. Why did it happen and what can be learnt from it?
2 **Why is this change necessary or desired?** If it is change being done to you, put yourself in their shoes and seek to understand why the change is necessary. Try to stay impersonal and objective, however hard this may be. If you are the one instigating the change, articulate why this change is the right thing to do.
3 **Broader trends.** What broad trends are happening that are relevant to the change in question? Changes to your industry, changes to the way work is done, changes to the way we live, changes to society… Make a list and do some research.

Outcomes

4 **What am I wanting to achieve?** What does good look like for me? What is the outcome I want – financial and non-financial? Is it just a job, any job? Or is it something more profound like being truly independent or doing a job that truly fulfils me? What am I really trying to achieve – longer term and at this point in my life/career?
5 **What are the implications of the change?** If I do achieve what I want to achieve what are the positive and negative consequences of this? For me? For my loved ones? What could I do to mitigate these implications?

SWOT

6 **What are my strengths?** What am I good at? What are my key skills? What do I excel at? What do I do better than most? (Be honest. In fact, get some input from trusted friends, colleagues or loved ones if you feel up to it!)
7 **What are my weaknesses?** What am I not so good at? Which weaknesses do I need to address? Which ones will I never be much good at? (After all, we can't be good at everything!) Which key skills should I improve/sharpen? What new skills should I try to develop? How?

NB: There are some 'weaknesses' that you shouldn't bother with addressing. I cannot see the point in wasting a great deal of time trying to improve a weakness at which you will simply never be very good, eg a weakness I have no desire to improve is the fact I am a terrible project manager. There is just no point in trying to turn me into one. Yes, I could certainly be more organized but I will never be a world-class PM. I always need to be teamed up with someone who is more process-focused than I am.

But a weakness I *can* work on is my tendency to worry too much about the future. I could achieve so much more by staying much longer in the present. That is something I *can* work to improve.

Another interesting thought is that our strongest strength is often also our strongest weakness – and vice versa. One of my key strengths is that I am good at getting along with people. I am personable and like to make people laugh. On the flip side, this can translate into an almost desperate need to be liked. It has also resulted in me occasionally not being taken as seriously as I would have liked. In business, particularly financial services, if you are smiling and have a penchant for laughter, this can be perceived as a lack of gravitas, a lack of professionalism. And laugh wrinkles. Loads of them.

What are your weaknesses?

8 **What are my opportunities?** What are the potential opportunities that you may be able to engineer or take advantage of? Make a list and return to it frequently during the analysis and action phases below.

9 **What are my threats?** If big change is being done to you, this will be easy. But it is good to be clear about them. What (external) threats could perhaps stand in your way? Write them down and understand them.

The situation

10 **Key success factors.** What are the most important things that I have to do, develop or put in place for this to be successful?

11 **Key challenges/obstacles to success.** What are the key barriers to success? What are my key emotional barriers to change? How will I overcome them?

12 **Interdependencies.** What key things do I need from others? How will I make sure I get them?

Action

13 **Preferences.** What do I like and what are my preferred no-go areas? A very good friend of mine has worked out that he simply hates working for himself. He hates the overt uncertainty of being self-employed. As a self-employed consultant, he was forever worrying about the future. During the good times, he was wondering what would happen at the end of the current contract and during the down times he was worrying about when the next one was going to come along. Even though loyalty in the workplace has been fading for many decades and one could argue that no job is 'safe' – he would opt for being an employee over being a contractor any day. That sort of thing is good to know.

14 **What are my options?** Then, armed with the above analysis, you can start to explore some potential future scenarios. When first compiling this list, don't bother yourself with how likely the scenario is – just whether it is plausible. Think of this exercise like an archery target; a bullseye. Start close to what you know and work outwards and see where it takes you.

So... let's say I am facing redundancy; what are my options? I could:

Future employer

- apply for another role in the same company (inner circle of the bullseye);
- apply to a competitor (moving one ring outwards);
- work for a supplier (a further ring);
- work for a customer/partner organization;
- work for a company/association with ties to my industry or one that services my industry (moving yet another ring away from the centre);
- work for a company trying to get into my industry;
- enter a completely new industry/area of work (I think we have just started a new bullseye with this one).

Location

- work near my current location;
- my current city/county;
- within two hours' commute;

- anywhere in the country;
- anywhere in the region;
- somewhere else in the world.

Type of work

- employee;
- self-employed;
- part-time;
- job-share.

What are the implications of each of the above?

Analysis of each option. Once you have made your list, you can then analyse each of the options – ask yourself, what are the key challenges, key opportunities and key consequences of each scenario?

But beware of paralysis by analysis. Having completed your analysis (and it doesn't need to be as detailed as the above!), at some point, you will have to make a decision. And when you do, be bold, make the leap and do your utmost to make it a success.

15 **Quick wins.** What short-term wins/milestones can I do to demonstrate a sense of achievement and momentum?

16 **Action plan and schedule.** So, what are you going to do, by when, in what sequence and when? It's time for action!

17 **Sustaining the change.** There will be hiccups along the way. The Change Curve will never be far away. What are you going to do to keep the momentum going?

Success often comes about after many setbacks.

And lastly, remember that success often comes about after many setbacks. Thomas Edison failed countless times before inventing the light bulb, although he saw it a little differently. When a reporter asked, 'How did it feel to fail 1,000 times?' Edison replied, 'I didn't fail 1,000 times. The light bulb was an invention with 1,000 steps'.

(A template of the above 'Personal Change Plan' can be downloaded at www.changeandstrategy.com.)

CHAPTER TWENTY-EIGHT

Be your own change leader

*True power
is living
the realization
that you are your own
healer, hero and leader.* YUNG PUEBLO[1]

In the end, it is up to you. It is up to you to be your own therapist; to be your own catalyst for change.

Yes, find people to help but know that in the end the responsibility is yours and yours alone. Even with their invaluable assistance, you will have to be the one to change. And to do that, you will need to be up for changing. Remember the old joke about social workers that I mentioned in the introduction: 'How many social workers does it take to change a light bulb? Only one, but the light bulb has got to want to change.'

It is up to you to be your own therapist; to be your own catalyst for change.

To lead yourself through this change, I suggest you reflect upon what makes for a successful change initiative. Below is the list I use for business leaders (it also happens to be the titles of chapters 11–20 of *The Change Catalyst*). It is a great checklist for personal change, too. After all, all change is personal.

The essential ingredients of successful (business) change:

1 complete clarity regarding what you are trying to achieve and why;
2 detailed understanding of the implications of the change;
3 laser-like focus on the outcomes;
4 a change process that includes a 'pause for reflection';
5 clear governance and thorough planning (set yourself up to succeed);
6 genuine engagement with people and influencers;
7 find (your) emotional triggers;
8 strong, committed, aligned and unwavering leadership team (that's you!);
9 a change-ready culture (surround yourself with people and attitudes that will help you make the change);
10 a change catalyst (that's you, too!).

Treating 'losing weight' as a change project

Let's apply the above principles to the personal challenge of losing weight. It will sound a bit corporate-ish, but it works.

By the way, please don't get the idea that I am obsessed with weight loss! Quite the opposite: an obsession with weight loss can be dangerous. It is just such a perfect example of personal change that almost all of us can identify with at some point in our lives.

1 **Clarity of what we are trying to achieve and why.** Why do you want to lose weight? Be open and honest. What's the 'right' reason you want to lose weight? What's the 'real' reason? The real reason will be the more compelling of the two. Write them all down. What are you trying to achieve? Why? Describe the end state you are looking for – in words and numbers (if you wish). Use the world 'sustainable' in there somewhere as this is about permanent change.
2 **Understand the implications of the change.** What will be the good implications of your successful weight loss? Will there be any negative consequences? (For example, some spouses and friends have not liked the lighter partner that emerged after losing weight.) Think about how to overcome the negative implications of your weight loss as well as embracing the positive consequences of the change.

3 **Laser-like focus on the outcomes.** Never take your eye off the goal if you want to achieve it. Now… that doesn't necessarily mean numbers. Numbers are not the answer for everyone. In fact, we can become obsessed with numbers. 'Oh no! I have gained 0.3 kg since yesterday morning!' After my BMI-induced attack of silliness mentioned in an earlier chapter, my daughter told me to throw away my scales. She has a point. Maybe a better description of success for me is that I would like to feel more comfortable in my suits; that I would like to feel healthier and have more energy. What would success look like for you? If numbers will help you achieve your goals, use them. Otherwise, a looser belt and a general feeling of wellbeing may be the best measurement of success.

4 **A change process that includes a 'pause for reflection'.** After a few weeks, pause and reflect: are my original objectives still valid? Why? Is this harder than I thought? Easier? What do I need to do differently? Should I be exercising more? Should I be exercising less? Is the new way of eating too restrictive to be sustainable? Or am I not taking it seriously enough? Stay objective; stay detached. This is not about judging yourself; it is about assessing progress and adjusting accordingly.

5 **Set your weight loss project up to succeed.** Remove obstacles to success (like fruit juice, cakes and biscuits). Set up your environment to succeed. Set realistic goals. Allow yourself to be kind to yourself. Like yourself through the process. Prepare the groundwork for success. Create new habits; new eating and exercise routines.

6 **Genuine engagement with stakeholders.** Be honest with yourself, with your family, with the people around you. Bring them onside; enlist their genuine and encouraging assistance. Make them part of the solution, not part of the problem. They will all want to help – and they won't judge either. They will think you are even more fabulous for doing this. (This doesn't have to be as melodramatic as it sounds! If your challenge is that you really like downing a few beers with neighbours at the local on a Friday night, your mates won't think any less of you if you stop at two… note to self.)

7 **Find your emotional triggers.** You know how you tick better than anyone else does. What will trigger your emotions to help you stay the course and embrace this new way of eating and living?

8 **Strong, committed leadership.** You are leading this change. Be empathetic to yourself but stay strong; stay committed.

9 **A change-ready culture.** In organizational change, culture is everything when it comes to change. Culture is how people behave. In point 6, you helped the people around you to understand. You also need them to behave in ways that will help you succeed. It's up to you to ensure they do. As the leader of this change project, you also need to set the tone. How you behave will determine how the people around you behave. If you are empathetic and confident, they will be too. If you treat this as an exciting challenge and stay committed, so will they. As your own change leader, you have to set the example.

10 **Be your own Change Catalyst.** You can be your own catalyst for change. Everything you need to change is inside of you already. Your inner Change Catalyst needs to stay focused on the outcomes and continually monitor each step above – ensuring that everything is in place for you to achieve long-term, sustainable success.

Even though I originally developed this approach for use in organizational change, it is adaptable and relevant to any instance of personal change.

PART SIX

The secrets to embracing change

And now we come to the part of the book where we wrap it all up into a neat bow and we summarize the secrets to successfully embracing change.

Before we go there, let me stress that everybody's appetite for embracing change is different – and it varies from one situation to the next. Some changes we find ridiculously easy to embrace and adopt the new way of living or working. It's like riding a bicycle. Other changes feel more like trying to fly a jet fighter – we don't know where to start and find the whole thing utterly daunting.

But hopefully, among the many tips and techniques outlined in this book, you will find something that will help in almost any new situation. This isn't a manual on how to change. It is a series of hopefully enlightening insights, ideas and tools for you to choose from.

And the secret to embracing change? It lies between your ears. It lies inside your mind and your heart. You have it. We all do. We just need to find it and unleash it.

Change is inevitable and our ability to embrace it and look for the opportunities will underpin our future happiness and success – at work and in life.

CHAPTER TWENTY-NINE

The Embracing Change Checklist

Bad checklists are vague and imprecise. They are too long; they are hard to use; they are impractical. They treat the people using the tools as dumb and try to spell out every single step. Good checklists, on the other hand, are precise, efficient and to the point. They do not try to spell out everything – a checklist cannot fly a plane. Instead, they provide reminders of only the most critical and important steps. Good checklists are, above all, practical. ATUL GAWANDE[1] (Yes there is actually a book dedicated to checklists!)

Let's see if this Embracing Change Checklist lives up to Atul Gawande's high standards.

The secrets to embracing change are:

1 Accept that change is inevitable. It just is. End of.
2 Accept that not all change is going to be 'good'. But even 'bad' change needs to be embraced at some point so we can then start to look for the opportunities – and move on.
3 Understand that all change is emotional. Work out which emotional barriers you tend to erect and the tactics you need to adopt to overcome them.
4 Be detached. Detached from your negative thoughts, your emotions, your ego, your identity, your fears, your bad tribe.

5 Create favourable conditions for change. Be like the HENRY practitioners.

When big change arrives – even when it is forced upon you – remember that you are not powerless.

6 Be your own Change Catalyst. Your own consultant. Do your own analysis of the situation you are in, take stock of your personal strengths and build your own plan of action.

7 Help others. Helping others to navigate their way through change is not only a wonderful thing to do but it is also fantastic therapy for ourselves – and we usually learn as much, if not more, than the people we are helping.

8 It's about attitude. When big change arrives – even when it is forced upon you – remember that you are not powerless. Far from it. The one thing you can control is how you react. And this can make all the difference.

CHAPTER THIRTY

The power to change

Finally, in conclusion, let me just say this... PETER SELLERS[1]

Change is tough. It comes in many forms and it is relentless.

We started this tale with an exploration of just some of the macro changes heading our way. Technology is advancing so rapidly that our governments and our societies are struggling to keep pace. The way we work, the way we live, even how long we live are all changing forever – in ways that are dramatic and fundamental.

Those of us who can cope with the changes ahead will survive. Those of us who can embrace the change and seek out the opportunities will thrive. Embracing change is the most important skill that any of us can

Embracing change is the most important skill that any of us can hone.

hone. And the power to do just that is contained within every single one of us.

We explored how all change is personal and all change is emotional. We touched upon the immense and often untapped power of the mind; how our mind can change our bodies; how it can change our destiny.

We discussed two different types of big, transformational change: 'Burning Platform' change that is done to us and 'Quantum Leap' change that we bring about ourselves. And how we react to both types of change is both highly emotional and completely predictable.

We travelled through the 'Burning Platform Change Curve', starting with Shock and Denial before moving on to Anger, Fear and Depression before we can move up the other side and get to Understanding, Acceptance and finally Moving On. We noted that the change curve is not one-way traffic. Neither is it a once-in-a-lifetime-experience. It is part of life. We need to study it, study ourselves and embrace it.

We spent quite a bit of time exploring life in the trough of the curve; the place where victims dwell. We discussed the insidious nature and cold comfort of victimhood – and how reframing the situation in our minds is the only way to escape.

We also discovered that we undergo a rollercoaster of emotions when it is 'good change' that we have chosen ourselves. 'Quantum Leap' change also has its own Change Curve that may be shallower but is not dissimilar to its steeper cousin. With change we have instigated, our reactions begin with Excitement but can also slide into Apprehension, Fear and a form of Remorse before our head helps Rational Optimism to begin and our heart then starts to genuinely believe that we can thrive in the new world and we are able to fully embrace the change.

But no matter what type of change confronts us, we are not powerless. How we choose to react to the change is completely within our control – and this choice can make all the difference.

We explored the key personal barriers that we erect to change in some detail, along with ways to overcome them.

Within this book, we learnt to admit denial, test our doubts, find good tribes, reframe our identity, find our own emotional triggers and 'choose our attitude'. We discussed how all fear is fear of the future and how to lessen our key fears when it comes to change: fear of failure, fear of blame and fear of the unknown.

We learnt to treat our thoughts and beliefs for what they are – stories, to stop judging ourselves and that we have the ability to tell ourselves new stories – to change our thoughts and challenge our beliefs.

We discussed how yoga is brilliant for helping us to declutter, reset our minds and welcome the change.

But most all, we learnt that we could be our own catalyst for change.

We then explored six additional skills, tips and strategies for embracing change:

1 resilience;
2 creating favourable conditions for change;
3 finding the help you need;
4 helping others;
5 my personal change plan;
6 be your own change leader.

Another key theme that runs throughout the book is that no-one embraces change simply because they are told to do so. We only change if we want to. Therefore, we must help ourselves to want to change.

I hope you enjoyed the book as much as I did writing it.

To get in touch, to download any of the templates or to view videos, download podcasts or subscribe to my newsletter, visit www.changeandstrategy.com.

> *No-one embraces change simply because they are told to do so.*

It is not the strongest of the species that survive, nor the most intelligent, but the one most responsive to change. CHARLES DARWIN[2]

Notes

Part One Foreword

1 Benjamin Disraeli, 1st Earl of Beaconsfield, KG, PC, FRS (1804–81) was a British politician and writer, who twice served as Prime Minister
2 *B-b-b-b-b-baby, you aint seen n-n-n-n-nothing yet*, Bachman Turnover Overdrive, 1974

Chapter One

1 The Washington Post [accessed 12 March 2020] Fact Checker database [Online] www.washingtonpost.com/news/fact-checker (archived at https://perma.cc/E59X-C3X3)
2 A well-known quote with an unknown provenance often attributed to Nazi Propaganda Minister, Josef Goebbels
3 R Kurzweil (2006) *The Singularity is Near: When humans transcend biology*, Penguin Books, London
4 Greg Hayes, Chief Executive of United Technologies, owner of Carrier Air-Conditioning, in an interview with CNN, 8 December 2016

Chapter Two

1 L Gratton (2017) *The 100-Year Life: Living and working in an age of longevity*, Bloomsbury, London
2 WHO (2006) [accessed 12 March 2020] Health, history and hard choices: Funding dilemmas in a fast-changing world, *World Health Organization: Thomason Prentice Global Health Histories* [Online] www.who.int/global_health_histories/seminars/presentation07.pdf (archived at https://perma.cc/W3YP-85W7)

3   Seniorliving.org [accessed 12 March 2020] 1900–2000: Changes in life expectancy in the United States [Online] www.seniorliving.org/history/1900-2000-changes-life-expectancy-united-states/ (archived at https://perma.cc/8LA4-DE2U)

4   Worldlifeexpectancy.com [accessed 12 March 2020] Life expectancy white American male [Online] www.worldlifeexpectancy.com/usa/life-expectancy-white-male (archived at https://perma.cc/6TLC-U4SM)

5   Worldpopulationreview.com [accessed 12 March 2020] Life Expectancy by Country 2017 [Online] worldpopulationreview.com/countries/life-expectancy (archived at https://perma.cc/W45N-X2PJ)

6   US Department of Health & Human Services (2012) [accessed 12 March 2020] A profile of older Americans [Online] acl.gov/aging-and-disability-in-america/data-and-research/profile-older-americans (archived at https://perma.cc/9FWK-JUJ7)

7   *The Independent* (2016) [accessed 12 March 2020] Figures from the Human Mortality Database [Online] https://mortality.org/ (archived at https://perma.cc/RU7K-5824)

8   L Dwyer-Lindgren, A Bertozzi-Villa and R W Stubbs (2017) [accessed 12 March 2020] Inequalities in life expectancy among US counties, 1980 to 2014: Temporal trends and key drivers [Online] https://jamanetwork.com/journals/jamainternalmedicine/fullarticle/2626194 (archived at https://perma.cc/GX7P-4KN5)

9   S Adams (2012) [accessed 12 March 2020] Obesity killing three times as many as malnutrition, *Telegraph* [Online] www.telegraph.co.uk/news/health/news/9742960/Obesity-killing-three-times-as-many-as-malnutrition.html (archived at https://perma.cc/5DXR-QBVH)

10 Global Health Observatory data 2012, World Health Organization via Yuval Noah Harari (2017) *Homo Deus: A brief history of tomorrow,* Vintage

11 Calico [accessed 12 March 2020] Website, www.calicolabs.com (archived at https://perma.cc/U2VR-77XF)

Chapter Three

1   American Meteorological Society (2018) [accessed 12 March 2020] The 28th annual 'State of the Climate' report [Online] www.ametsoc.org/index.cfm/ams/publications/bulletin-of-the-american-meteorological-society-bams/state-of-the-climate/ (archived at https://perma.cc/L9RH-DDNC)

2   Smithsonian (2018) [accessed 12 March 2020] Sea level rise [Online] https://ocean.
    si.edu/through-time/ancient-seas/sea-level-rise (archived at https://perma.cc/
    B64M-C5W7)

3   NASA (2018) [accessed 12 March 2020] New study finds sea level rise accelerating
    [Online] https://climate.nasa.gov/news/2680/new-study-finds-sea-level-rise-
    accelerating/ (archived at https://perma.cc/79DL-YPWY)

Chapter Four

1   Inspirational founder of The Ocean Cleanup

2   The Ocean Cleanup [accessed 17 March 2020] Website, www.theoceancleanup.com
    (archived at https://perma.cc/M3L3-PLLL)

3   Study led by Dr Jenna Jambeck of the University of Georgia, the results of which
    were announced at the 2015 American Association for the Advancement of Science
    (AAAS) Annual Meeting

4   NRDC [accessed 17 March 2020] Website, www.nrdc.org (archived at https://
    perma.cc/B6AV-UV93)

5   S Smillie [accessed 17 March 2020] From sea to plate: How plastic got into fish,
    The Guardian [Online] www.theguardian.com/lifeandstyle/2017/feb/14/sea-to-plate-
    plastic-got-into-fish (archived at https://perma.cc/CLQ5-2DFU)

6   The Ocean Cleanup [accessed 17 March 2020] Website, www.theoceancleanup.com
    (archived at https://perma.cc/M3L3-PLLL)

7   B Cenkus [accessed 17 March 2020] Millennials will work hard, just not for your
    crappy job, The Startup [Online] https://medium.com/swlh/millennials-will-work-
    hard-just-not-for-your-crappy-job-82c12a1853ed (archived at https://perma.cc/
    PH64-ANKN)

8   Courtesy of Economic Policy Unit Report by A Davis and L Mishel [accessed 17
    March 2020] CEO pay continues to rise as typical workers are paid less [Online]
    www.epi.org/publication/ceo-pay-continues-to-rise/ (archived at https://perma.cc/
    Q86F-5SSM)

Chapter Five

1   Author of *Sapiens*, *Homo Deus* and *21 Lessons for the 21st Century* in a BBC
    Radio 4 interview 1 October 2018

2   Office of National Statistics

3 A Kirk [accessed 17 March 2020] How Britain's self-employed army are keeping our economy afloat, *The Telegraph* [Online] www.telegraph.co.uk/news/2017/03/10/britains-self-employed-army-keeping-economy-afloat/ (archived at https://perma.cc/L7SB-EQNE)

4 A Monaghan [accessed 17 March 2020] Self-employment in UK at highest level since records began, *The Guardian* [Online] www.theguardian.com/uk-news/2014/aug/20/self-employment-uk-highest-level (archived at https://perma.cc/9924-4P24)

5 C Macpherson (2017) *The Change Catalyst*, Wiley, London

Part Two Foreword

1 Roman Emperor AD 161–180

Chapter Six

1 S Fischer [accessed 17 March 2020] Tap the placebo effect to unlock your body's healing powers, *New Scientist* [Online] www.newscientist.com/article/2079643-tap-the-placebo-effect-to-unlock-your-bodys-healing-powers/ (archived at https://perma.cc/9PCS-VT3U)

2 WebMD [accessed 17 March 2020] Website, www.webmd.com (archived at https://perma.cc/GWH2-QQL4)

3 1743–1826. US Founding Father, 3rd US President and author of the *Declaration of Independence*

Chapter Eight

1 D Carnegie (1936) *How to Win Friends and Influence People*, Simon and Schuster, New York

2 Professor of Neuroscience at the University of Southern California and an Adjunct Professor at the Salk Institute

3 Global Health Observatory data 2012 via Yuval Noah Harari's *Homo Deus* (2016)

4 JD Vance (2016) *Hillbilly Elegy: A memoir of a family and culture in crisis*, Harper & Row, New York

Part Three Foreword

1   Greek Philosopher AD 55–135

Chapter Nine

1   Italian polymath and Renaissance Man (1452–1519). His areas of interest included invention, drawing, painting, sculpting, architecture, science, music, mathematics, engineering, literature, anatomy, geology, astronomy, botany, writing, history and cartography. He has been variously called the father of palaeontology, ichnology and architecture, and he is widely considered one of the greatest painters of all time.

Chapter Ten

1   Swiss-American psychiatrist and inventor of The Change Curve (1926–2004)
2   American author of 1970s best-sellers, including *Jonathan Livingston Seagull* (1970) and *Illusions: The adventures of a reluctant messiah* (1977)
3   US life coach
4   S Karpman (1968) Fairy tales and script drama analysis, *Transactional Analysis Bulletin*, 7 (26), pp 39–43. In 1968, Stephen Karpman, MD invented what he called 'The Drama Triangle', also known as 'The Victim Triangle', to map 'transactions' in conflicted or drama-intense relationship situations
5   D Emerald Womeldorff (2016) *The Power of TED: The Empowerment Dynamic*, 10th anniversary edition, Polaris, Edinburgh

Chapter Eleven

1   A closely-linked group of 24 universities across the UK regarded by many private schools to be the leading group of universities. What is interesting is the top-class universities that have not joined The Russell Group – Bath, Sussex, St Andrews, Strathclyde, Surrey, Loughborough...

Chapter Thirteen

1   Marie Curie (1867–1934) was a Polish and naturalized-French physicist and chemist who conducted pioneering research on radioactivity. She was the first woman to win a Nobel Prize, the first person and only woman to win twice, and the only person to win a Nobel Prize in two different sciences. She died age 66 of aplastic anaemia from exposure to radiation.

2   WHO [accessed 17 March 2020] Tobacco [Online] www.who.int/news-room/fact-sheets/detail/tobacco (archived at https://perma.cc/PZ3K-FS8E)

3   A Uribe [accessed 17 March 2020] Australian super funds ascendant in global rankings, *Investment Magazine* [Online] www.investmentmagazine.com.au/2018/09/australian-super-funds-ascendant-in-global-rankings/ (archived at https://perma.cc/62AQ-ATPH)

4   G Haigh [accessed 17 March 2020] The doctor who beat big tobacco, *The Guardian* [Online] www.theguardian.com/news/2016/aug/01/the-doctor-who-beat-big-tobacco (archived at https://perma.cc/YL3T-7JMK)

5   G Haigh [accessed 17 March 2020] The doctor who beat big tobacco, *The Guardian* [Online] www.theguardian.com/news/2016/aug/01/the-doctor-who-beat-big-tobacco (archived at https://perma.cc/YL3T-7JMK)

6   Neil Woodford, cited in G Haigh [accessed 17 March 2020] The doctor who beat big tobacco, *The Guardian* [Online] www.theguardian.com/news/2016/aug/01/the-doctor-who-beat-big-tobacco (archived at https://perma.cc/YL3T-7JMK) – Neil Woodford, once the UK's 'rockstar' fund manager, made a great deal of money from tobacco stocks during his glory days

7   ILO [accessed 17 March 2020] ILO cooperation with the tobacco industry in the pursuit of the Organization's social mandate [Online] www.ilo.org/wcmsp5/groups/public/---ed_norm/---relconf/documents/meetingdocument/wcms_545944.pdf (archived at https://perma.cc/8T47-44ED)

8   H Cox [accessed 17 March 2020] The future of tobacco may be going up in smoke, *The Times* [Online] www.thetimes.co.uk/edition/money/the-future-of-tobacco-may-be-going-up-in-smoke-pnvp0jtrv (archived at https://perma.cc/45E6-3QEG)

9   S Hawthorne [accessed 17 March 2020] Nest to divest all tobacco holdings, *Pensions Expert* [Online] www.pensions-expert.com/Investment/Nest-to-divest-all-tobacco-holdings?ct=true (archived at https://perma.cc/4BV2-C2JJ)

10 The WHO estimates that global prevalence of tobacco smoking has decreased from 26.9 per cent of people aged 15 and over in 2000 to 20.2 per cent in 2015

11 BAT [accessed 17 March 2020] Website, www.bat.com (archived at https://perma.cc/8RJ3-J3XX)

12 Although Imperial has recently abandoned its policy of increasing its annual dividend by 10 per cent every year as its share price 'has been struggling against a trend towards ethical investment – pushing some investors to offload tobacco stocks – and market worries about a crackdown on e-cigarettes in the US'. F Washtell [accessed 17 March 2020] Imperial Brands to abandon long-running policy of hiking dividends by 10% a year, as it fights fears that it's unsustainable, *This is Money* [Online] www.thisismoney.co.uk/money/markets/article-7225849/Imperial-Brands-abandon-long-running-policy-hiking-dividend-10pc-year-2020.html (archived at https://perma.cc/SUL7-ZLN4)

13 R Eccles [accessed 17 March 2020] Solving the Cigarette Problem [Online] www.linkedin.com/pulse/solving-cigarette-problem-robert-eccles/ (archived at https://perma.cc/35GT-6NYX)

14 Foundation for a Smoke-Free World [accessed 17 March 2020] Website, www.smokefreeworld.org/our-vision (archived at https://perma.cc/4WJU-FPW9)

15 V da Costa e Silva [accessed 17 March 2020] Engagement with tobacco industry conflicting with UN principles and values [Online] www.who.int/fctc/secretariat/head/statements/2017/ungc-integrity-review-tobacco-industry/en/ (archived at https://perma.cc/XG89-S4HD)

16 Wikipedia [accessed 17 March 2020] Electronic cigarette [Online] https://en.m.wikipedia.org/wiki/Electronic_cigarette (archived at https://perma.cc/5JDP-68GD)

17 M Blaha [accessed 17 March 2020] 5 vaping facts you need to know [Online] www.hopkinsmedicine.org/health/wellness-and-prevention/5-truths-you-need-to-know-about-vaping (archived at https://perma.cc/B4UK-2SZN)

Chapter Fourteen

1 US writer who specialized in mystery and the macabre (1809–49)

Part Four Foreword

1 Charles Franklin Kettering (1876–1958) was a US inventor, engineer, businessman, and the holder of 186 patents

Chapter Fifteen

1 B Kortenbach (2013) *Counterpredators: Survival Response Conditioning and the Parent/Child Connection*, eBookIt.com

Chapter Sixteen

1 South African human behaviour specialist
2 Corporate Leadership Council, part of the Corporate Executive Board, now part of Gartner Group, list of libraries with copy [accessed 17 March 2020] Driving employee performance and retention through employee engagement [Online] www.worldcat.org/title/driving-employee-performance-and-retention-through-engagement-a-quantitative-analysis-of-the-effectiveness-of-employee-engagement-strategies/oclc/57470164 (archived at https://perma.cc/5FQA-HAT5)
3 US poet, singer, memoirist and civil rights activist (1928–2014)

Chapter Seventeen

1 Marie Curie (1867–1934) was a Polish and naturalized French physicist and chemist who conducted pioneering research on radioactivity. She was the first woman to win a Nobel Prize, the first person and only woman to win twice, and the only person to win a Nobel Prize in two different sciences. She died age 66 of aplastic anaemia from exposure to radiation
2 R Moss Kanter (2012) [accessed 19 March 2020] Ten reasons people resist change, *Harvard Business Review* [Online] https://hbr.org/2012/09/ten-reasons-people-resist-chang (archived at https://perma.cc/Z93Z-TDPT)
3 US actor and musician (1925–2001). Lemmon was an eight-time Academy Award nominee, with two wins
4 US motivational speaker, writer and consultant, born 1933
5 T N Rogers (2018) [accessed 19 March 2020] Billionaire Spanx founder Sara Blakely has a simple piece of advice for single women dreading the marriage question at Thanksgiving: Be the CEO your parents want you to marry, *Business Insider* [Online] www.businessinsider.sg/spanx-billionaire-sara-blakely-tip-for-single-women-at-thanksgiving-2019-11 (archived at https://perma.cc/K373-7EKB)
6 D Stone (1999) *Difficult Conversations: How to discuss what matters most*, Penguin, London

7   Thich Nhat Hahn, Thai Buddhist Monk, Teacher and International Peace Activist (2012) *You Are Here: Discover the magic of the present moment*, Shambhala Publications, Boulder, CO

8   E Cleaver (1935–98), a US political activist who was talking about getting engaged in the US civil rights movement. To Eldridge, being passive was equivalent to working against the cause

9   US author (1890–1937) who achieved posthumous fame through his influential works of horror fiction

10 Francis Bacon, 1st Viscount St Alban, PC QC (1561–1626) was an English philosopher and statesman who served as Attorney General and as Lord Chancellor of England. He is credited with developing the scientific method

11 Lord Ashcroft poll of 12,369 people on the day of the referendum

12 Mingyur Rinpoche (1975) is a Tibetan teacher and master of the Karma Kagyu and Nyingma lineages of Tibetan Buddhism. He has authored two best-selling books and oversees the Tergar Meditation Community, an international network of Buddhist meditation centres

13 Netflix's 'Mind Explained' episode on Mindfulness

Chapter Eighteen

1   Professor Emeritus in Psychiatry, University of California

2   S Sloman and P Fernbach (2017) *The Knowledge Illusion: Why we never think alone*, Riverhead, New York

3   Christopher Peterson (1950–2012) was the Arthur F. Thurnau Professor of Psychology at the University of Michigan and co-founder of positive psychology

Chapter Nineteen

1   Genevan philosopher, writer and composer (1712–78)

Chapter Twenty

1   Bertrand Russell (1872–1970) was a British philosopher, logician, mathematician, historian, writer, essayist, social critic, political activist and Nobel laureate

2   Theologian Reinhold Niebuhr (1892–1971) first wrote the prayer for a sermon at Heath Evangelical Union Church in Massachusetts, USA

Chapter Twenty-one

1 British illusionist extraordinaire from his show *Miracle* available on Netflix
2 1856–1941. US lawyer and associate justice on the Supreme Court of the United States from 1916 to 1939
3 These two philosophies are slightly revised versions of the first two 'yamas', the philosophical guidelines that underpin yoga and a lesser-known religion called Jainism, which given my wife's occupation and name seem spookily appropriate!
4 US author (1898–1993) of *The Power of Positive Thinking* (1952, Prentice Hall, Upper Saddle River, NJ)

Chapter Twenty-two

1 Bellur Krishnamachar Sundararaja Iyengar (1918–2014) was the founder of the style of modern yoga known as 'Iyengar Yoga' and was considered one of the foremost yoga teachers in the world. In 2004, Iyengar was named one of the 100 most influential people in the world by *Time* magazine
2 Patanjali is the name of the author (possibly more than one) of ancient Sanskrit texts including the definitive text on yoga theory and practice, the Yoga Sutras, some time between the 2nd century BC and the 4th century AD
3 Michael was an incredible mindfulness teacher whose life was cut short in 2017. His teachings live on through the website michaelstoneteaching.com. To quote his website: 'He continues through his teachings, his children, the three people who received his organs, and those who loved him. He is loved immeasurably'
4 The 'Father of Medicine' and the Ancient Greek physician after whom the Hippocratic Oath is named, the oath still taken by doctors worldwide today (460–370 BC)

Chapter Twenty-three

1 Nelson Mandela (1918–2013) was a South African anti-apartheid revolutionary, political leader and philanthropist who served as President of South Africa from 1994 to 1999. He was the country's first black head of state and the first elected in a fully representative democratic election
2 This hierarchy suggests that people are motivated to fulfil basic needs before moving on to other more advanced needs

3   'Inside Quest' interview with Simon Sinek, author of *Start with Why* (2009, Portfolio Books, New York) and other best-sellers, recorded in December 2016

4   I loathe the term 'politically correct'. It is too often used as an insult by people who are trying to mask their own prejudices. 'It's not politically correct to make jokes about gay people anymore; it's not politically correct to say that men make better business leaders; it's not politically correct to point out the differences between races.' Actually, just take the word 'politically' out of each of these sentences. It's just not correct. It has nothing to do with politics

5   Simon Sinek, author of *Start with Why* (2009, Portfolio Books, New York) and other best-sellers, recorded in December 2016

6   Such a strange saying. Instead of 'oyster', I have always said 'the world is your *lobster*, which makes even less sense. Unfortunately, my clever daughter grew up only hearing my version. She also seemed to have grown up pronouncing 'picturesque' as 'pictureskew'. Trusting soul that she is

7   'Inside Quest' interview with Simon Sinek, author of *Start with Why* (2009, Portfolio Books, New York) and other best-sellers, recorded in December 2016

8   The American Psychological Association (APA) reports that the primary factor in resilience is having caring and supportive relationships within and outside the family. Relationships that create love and trust provide role models and offer encouragement and reassurance that help bolster a person's resilience

9   Gordon Gecko in Oliver Stone (dir.) *Wall Street*, 1987

10 American Psychological Association (APA) [accessed 23 March 2020] Building your resilience [Online] www.apa.org/helpcenter/road-resilience (archived at https://perma.cc/CCP2-KDQY)

11 Mayo Clinic [accessed 23 March 2020] Build skills to endure hardship [Online] www.mayoclinic.org/tests-procedures/resilience-training/in-depth/resilience/art-20046311 (archived at https://perma.cc/5X3F-4A3C)

Chapter Twenty-four

1   HENRY [accessed 23 March 2020] Website, www.henry.org.uk (archived at https://perma.cc/R5E2-MW88)

2   HENRY Practitioner Manual, chapter 2

Chapter Twenty-five

1 US actress 1942–2013
2 LJ Peter and R Hull (1970) *The Peter Principle: Why things always go wrong*, Pan Books, London. The central premise of the book is that all managers are eventually promoted to their level of incompetence to stay there for the remainder of their careers, thus reaching their 'Peter Plateau'. A cynical view without doubt, but not entirely inaccurate
3 A parenting and lifestyle blog from a couple of parents in Brighton, UK [accessed 23 March 2020] Blog, www.fizzypeaches.com (archived at https://perma.cc/YP3K-TZPY)

Chapter Twenty-six

1 US businessman, speaker and politician (1945–)
2 Mentalfloss.com [accessed 23 March 2020] 7 scientific benefits of helping others [Online] http://mentalfloss.com/article/71964/7-scientific-benefits-helping-others (archived at https://perma.cc/56NY-HXHY)
3 Mentalfloss.com [accessed 23 March 2020] 7 scientific benefits of helping others [Online] http://mentalfloss.com/article/71964/7-scientific-benefits-helping-others (archived at https://perma.cc/56NY-HXHY)
4 C Ryan Hyde (1999) *Pay it Forward*, Simon and Schuster, New York
5 Pay it Forward Foundation [accessed 23 March 2020] Website, www.payitforwardfoundation.org (archived at https://perma.cc/5BM4-5DTD)
6 English American poet (1907–73)

Chapter Twenty-seven

1 Ancient Greek philosopher and 'Father of Western Philosophy' (384–322 BC)

Chapter Twenty-eight

1 Y Pueblo (2017) *Inward*, CreateSpace. 'A collection of poetry and prose that explores the movement from self-love to unconditional love, the power of letting go, and the wisdom that comes when we truly try to know ourselves' (Amazon)

Chapter Twenty-nine

1 A Gawande (2009) *The Checklist Manifesto,* Metropolitan Books, New York

Chapter Thirty

1 Comic genius and actor. *The Goon Show, The Pink Panther, The Party, Dr Strangelove, What's New Pussycat, Being There...* (1925–80)
2 English naturalist, father of the science of evolution and author of *On the Origin of Species* (1809–82)

Index

Wilson, Peter 53–54
work 33–37
  personal change plan 189–93
work–life balance 31, 176
World Health Organization 50
World War II 171–72
Wozniak, Steve 160

xenophobia 137–39
Xi Jinping 14

Ying Ao 14
yoga 3, 82, 112, 163–67
  principles 164–65

Zawistowski, Stephanie 27